THE WORD OF MOUTH MANUAL

Volume II

The Word of Mouth Manual
Volume II

Dave Balter

The Word of Mouth Manual, Volume II
Copyright © 2008 by Dave Balter

No part of this book may be reproduced without
written permission from the author. All requests
should be sent to BzzAgent, Inc.
500 Harrison Avenue
Boston, MA 02118
WOMII@bzzagent.com

Developed with *The* Butman Company *Inc.*

Produced by Print Matters, Inc.
Illustrations by Seth B. Minkin
Design by Amelia Costigan

ISBN 978-0-9796685-1-7

First Edition

CONTENTS

A few things you should know before reading this book

- There has been quite a bit of controversy around managed word of mouth, which I recognize and understand. There are some who still are genuinely concerned about this concept, but I truly believe that most of their worries are based on false assumptions, lack of information, others' long-standing errors, or superstition.

- I sincerely, genuinely, and completely believe that word of mouth is an incredibly powerful medium that is especially important today and that the "natural" kind of word of mouth really can't be and won't be compromised by the various new forms it has taken.

- This book is intended for several audiences: word of mouth practitioners and participants, so they can better understand and celebrate their medium; traditional marketers and advertisers who are trying to truly understand word of mouth and know they must do so in order to evolve, adapt, and succeed; and the general public, who live by word of mouth every day whether they realize it not.

- The book is divided into three sections. Part I: What You Should Know (in Theory) explores the most recent learnings and ideas about word of mouth. Part II: What You Probably Know Already (Unless You Don't) addresses those repetitive questions, doubts, and criticisms that emerged in the earliest stages of managed word of mouth and have now been answered. Part III: What You Must Know (in Practice) is about the essential elements that must be considered before practicing the medium.

- All of the artwork in the book as well as the cover illustration was created by Seth B. Minkin (www.sethbminkin.com), BzzAgent's artist-in-residence, who continues to make us cringe and laugh with every stroke of his paintbrush.

- Very special thanks to an incredible thought partner and friend, John Butman (www.ideaplatforms.com), who edited this book, helped refine the vision, and packaged it into something . . . well . . . worth talking about.

I. WHAT YOU SHOULD KNOW
(IN THEORY)

If you were suffering from a bad fever

in Europe in 1850, the cure might seem worse than the ailment. The doctor would arrive, possibly bespectacled and probably frazzled, open his satchel, pull out a jar filled with muddy water, extract from it a handful of leeches, and confidently place them on your fever-wracked body. There each leech would open wide its semicircular jaw, make a neat incision in your skin, excrete a bit of mucous, and begin sucking your blood.

The practice had been going on for 2,000 years or so, because it was thought to be an effective way to extract poisons from the system. In the late 1800s, due mainly to a lack of supply, the use of leeches tapered off. As we entered the 20th-century, many patients (and doctors) began to doubt that the leech approach was a good one.

However, in the last 25 years medical professionals have begun to reevaluate the power of the leech. It seems that its saliva contains an anesthetic and anticoagulant that can be very useful, especially during the surgical reattachment of things like chopped-off fingers, detached toes, and bitten-off ears.

Those 19th century doctors knew, by instinct and through practice, that they were on to something with leeches. They just weren't quite sure what. It wasn't until a century later that their hunches were finally validated.

1. 100% Pure, Unadulterated, Uncut, Straight-to-the-Vein, Word of Mouth Purity

THERE IS A SPECIAL type of word of mouth that is achieved by only a handful of products and a tiny fraction of the world's companies. And, in all likelihood, you don't have it.

What you're seeking is *pure* word of mouth.

It's the kind of evangelist eruption and wildfire opinion–spreading that happens only once or twice per decade. Suddenly, a brand that yesterday was almost invisible is recognized by every consumer from Boston to Bangkok. People want it so badly they line up on cold, dirty sidewalks, sleeping in their own grime and fervor for days on end in hopes of getting at least a glimpse of its greatness, even if it will be gone by the time they actually get to the store.

This kind of word of mouth, pure as the driven snow, makes all those clever little marketing tricks look irrelevant. Pricing and promotions? Endcaps and shelf talkers? Pop ups and scavenger hunts? With pure word of mouth driving sales, you could hide the product on the bottom shelves at a second-tier department store, price it at triple what it's worth, and it would still vanish. Pure word of mouth is what enables products to create an entire category, produce an evolution in the way we think, dress, or act, and even define a generation.

That's why marketers want so desperately to create it. Virtually every Fortune 500 company, at some point in its history, has thrown gobs of money at every kind of channel and media and gimmick—pumping messages online, offline, at events, in-store, outdoor, on handsets, across foreheads—trying to get some of that pure, unadulterated, straight-to-the-vein word of mouth for their beloved product.

By day, these marketers mobilize every strategy, tactic, process, and practice—whiteboarding, brainstorming, group snowboarding, Ouija channeling, trust falling, SWOT analyzing, and 2x2 matrixing—in search of discovering the Holy Grail of word of mouth. By night, they lie awake, tossing and turning, hoping and praying that their brand has whatever it takes to do whatever is required to reach the tipping point.

But, I'm sorry to say, all their efforts are futile.

Pure word of mouth cannot be deliberately created, intentionally generated, or purposefully harnessed. It's like trying to be a beat poet without graceful timing. Either you have rhythm or you don't.

What makes pure word of mouth so elusive?

It's the kind of natural phenomenon that occurs only when a number of factors come together in just the right way at just the right moment: beliefs, wants, habits, events, weather, and constellations. Suddenly, the entire cosmos is calling out to people, it's TIME!

No one can forecast when this moment will arrive. Pure word of mouth isn't accomplished—it's granted to the lucky chosen few. It's as unpredictable as when one presidential candidate will catch fire and leap from has-been to frontrunner or when a slumping baseball slugger will miraculously break out of the doldrums and go on a hitting streak like the game has never seen ('roids-free, of course).

This doesn't mean that marketers don't have the ability to make their brands sing or enable word of mouth as a trusted marketing outlet. Hardly. But even if they do have marketing skills akin to Julia Child's cooking abilities or Michael Jordan's dribbling prowess, it still doesn't mean they have the extrasensory perception, telekinesis, or precognition necessary to whip up pure word of mouth.

The story of Tickle Me Elmo gives you an idea of what pure word of mouth looks like.

Early in the morning of December 14, 1996, some 300 consumers stormed into a Wal-Mart in Fredericton, New Brunswick, hoping to get their hands on the must-have doll for their darling children for the upcoming holiday. Things turned ugly very fast. The last doll in stock, as fate would have it, was in the hands of a befuddled store employee. The rabid mob attacked him, knocked him to the floor, and wrestled the doll out of his grip. The poor guy suffered broken ribs and a concussion (not to mention a case of severely wounded pride).

Yes, the genius company that created Tickle Me Elmo—Tyco—

had spent millions on promoting the $30 doll. Certainly, their efforts helped fuel initial customer demand. But we all know that marketing is not what drove parents to pay black market prices of $1,500 or more to get their hands on a red plush creature that giggles when you poke it.

So what creates this type of customer volatility and aggression? Marketing theorists will point to psychological concepts like Maslow's hierarchy of needs. They'll tell you that this little red, chuckling doll climbed the needs pyramid to make it into the category of Esteem (just above Love/Belonging and just below Self-Actualization). These dolls came to represent achievement, brought people recognition, helped them feel accepted, and increased their feelings of self-worth.

C'mon . . . .

I'm sure most parents would agree that self-esteem had nothing to do with it. They just wanted to make their kid happy, and Tickle Me Elmo was a surefire way to do it.

Crocs, the brightly colored plastic clogs, is another brand that reached a peak of pure word of mouth madness. Crocs were developed as a boating/outdoor shoe with a slip-resistant, non-marking sole. It is, quite possibly, the ugliest looking lump of footwear ever designed, and comes in an equally hideous range of livid colors, including grape, cotton candy, fuchsia, celery, and sea foam.

The Crocs brand managers had a small marketing budget, but

slowly built acceptance and then passion among specific consumer segments—particularly sailors and nurses—who were
zealous about the performance and comfort of the shoes. The
brand gained an audience over a few years, but it also created an
intense negative reaction in some. Many people absolutely despised
Crocs, and loudly proclaimed their loathing on websites such as
www.ihatecrocs.com. *Maxim* magazine ranked Crocs #6 on its list
of the 10 worst things to happen to men's fashion in 2007.

Then, suddenly it seemed, everything clicked. Crocs became
the must-have, must-be-seen-in product of 2007. The time in the
market was just right. There was a dedicated fan base and a story
to tell. Almost everyone found a use for Crocs, from outfitting
their kids with an easy-to-put-on-and-even-easier-to-wash product
to gardening to pool lounging.

No other shoe in this category was being talked about. Who could
have predicted that comfortable ugliness would become the rage?

Marketers study pure word of mouth winners like Elmo and Crocs
and try to analyze their success. They identify the key components:

- STELLAR PRODUCT. Distinctive. Innovative. Features unlike
  anything else on the market.
- PASSIONATE AND DEDICATED CORE AUDIENCE. Made even more distinctive
  and noteworthy by a community of outspoken, equally passionate, product haters.

- **BRAND VALUES.** Consumers align with values that are very important to their own identity.
- **IMPECCABLE TIMING.** From youth trends to distribution to market demands to competitors' follies. The point: You can't pick this moment. It picks you.

But even in instances of pure word of mouth, marketing still plays a vital role. Tickle Me Elmo could not have been such a huge hit without the packaging that concealed the product, making the buyer desperate to get it home and rip open the box to get a look. Crocs sponsored the Association of Volleyball Professionals, an organization and cause as distinctive as the brand itself.

Most word of mouth is not so pure and, don't be disheartened, but your word of mouth is likely the other kind. It's more an intermittent rainstorm than a full-on hurricane. You're going to have to really work at it. Win people over slowly. You'll have occasional spikes in activity when all of the elements come together. You can generate more word of mouth if you focus, optimize, and pay attention to what your customers are asking of you—and it will be incredibly powerful for your brand, your product, and your sales.

But even with all that effort and attention, 99.999% of you will never achieve pure word of mouth. It's not that bad, really. The kind of word of mouth you *can* harness is still enough to convince Tickle Me Elmo to wear Crocs.

2. The Top 40 Products

IN JULY 1970, disc jockey Casey Kasem launched *American Top 40*, a radio show that played and tracked the 40 most popular songs in the United States. Millions of people tuned in and it soon became clear to musicians that getting on the list was a surefire way to get noticed and boost sales; for many it was the rocket they could ride to stardom.

Kasem spun the platters and between songs sprinkled bits of information about the artists and which tunes were climbing the chart fast and which were dropping like stones. It's fascinating to note (even if totally irrelevant to this book) that Ace of Base's "The Sign" remained in the #1 spot for 14 weeks in 1994, and still holds the record as the all-time longest consecutive weekly leader.

Recognizing the best of the best was more than just good programming—it became a harbinger of market trends. Today there are countdown lists for nearly everything you can imagine. *The Top 100 Childhood Stars* reminds you that Justin Henry was spectacular in the movie *Kramer vs. Kramer* as a 5-year-old who gets caught in the middle of an ugly divorce between his parents (played by Dustin Hoffman and Meryl Streep), and he entered manhood as the little brother of Molly Ringwald in *Sixteen Candles* ("Sofa City Sweetheart!"). If you can think of a category of anything, there is probably a Top list that tracks it: *Top 30 Car Chases Caught on Tape, Top 40 Girls of Rock, Top 10 Hollywood Disaster Stories.*

Kasem's genius lay in the commercialization of the Top 40 concept, which was actually conceived some 15 years earlier by Todd Storz, general manager of a collection of radio stations in Omaha, Nebraska. One night in 1955, Storz stopped into a bar for a drink or two. In those days, bars came equipped with that music-playing marvel known as a jukebox and, over the course of a couple of hours, Storz noticed something peculiar happening: the patrons of the bar kept playing a handful of songs from the jukebox, even though it offered a very wide selection.

Storz had never really thought about it before, but now became entranced by this behavior. He couldn't figure out why people would play a handful of songs over and over again rather than sample the whole catalog. After watching for a while, he concluded that the patrons of the bar were probably a pretty decent sample of the entire record-buying public. Did people only want to hear a small number of songs at any given time?

He decided to test the limited playlist idea at his radio stations and found that listeners tuned in more often when he played about 40 songs in the regular rotation.

Storz had unwittingly cracked the code of the behavior of the listening public. He had discovered that people are able to recognize—or actively remember—about 40 songs at any one time. Not many more. Not many less. Just about 40.

What Storz had recognized and what Kasem later turned into a marketing juggernaut was that narrowing the multitude of choices into a significant few was very valuable to people. So not only did *American Top 40* become an incredibly successful show, it also marked the beginning of our obsession with Top lists.

The significance of the Top 40, however, goes far beyond the hooks and rhythms of popular songs or the trends of popular culture—it applies to the ways in which we talk about all products and services. Each one of us carries around in our head about 40 products and services we're willing to talk about. If a product is on your personal Top 40 list, you become an engine that can help others know that product exists, driving credibility and sales. If a product doesn't make it on your list, you can bet every marketer on the planet wants to figure out how to get it there.

The power of important numbers isn't new when it comes to word of mouth theory. Malcolm Gladwell brought context to the concept of Dunbar's Number in his book, *The Tipping Point* where he noted that each of us has a social network capacity of about 150 people, and that number represents a boundary for how word of mouth spreads. Peeking under the hood of Dunbar's theory, there's a lot of jargon about brain neocortical processing capacity and ethnography, but the number itself is what's important: It presents the maximum number of direct routes each of us has to share our opinion with someone else.

But as every marketer knows, it doesn't matter if you have 150 friends or 1,500 if your product isn't one of those being talked about. That's what makes the idea of understanding the Top 40 list so important and powerful: It becomes the component for understanding the capacity for word of mouth for any person at any given time. If Dunbar's Number represented the entire national power grid, the Top 40 list would be the key generators that either light up the whole country or cause a blackout.

While it's unlikely that anyone would talk about all 40 products at one time (which would quickly reduce the number of friends willing to listen), the equation expresses the genetic code of the size of the entire word of mouth framework.

But beyond scope, the key questions remain: How does a product get on someone's Top 40 list? How often is it refreshed and updated? How do we use our list when talking with friends and family?

Your Top 40 list isn't the same as mine, and it's highly unlikely that it's like anyone else's. Like the pattern of a snowflake or the swirl of a thumbprint, no two are identical; they're each influenced by our experiences with products and services. For example, let's say you find yourself fiddling with a demo version of a digital video recorder (DVR) like TiVo at Circuit City. You have never experienced a DVR before, so the idea of being able to pause and record a live TV show completely shatters your conception of TV viewing. Your mind starts to race as you think about the implications of never having to fiddle with a VCR again, experiencing the joy of skipping commercials, and being able to automatically record *Bonanza* every morning at 2 A.M. instead of trying to stay awake for it.

Let's say you're a bit cautious and decide not to buy the DVR right then and there. You spend the next few days talking to other people about it. You chat with friends who own or have used similar products. You corner co-workers and ask their opinion. You check a blog that compares the capabilities of TiVo with competitive products and cable DVR systems.

What has happened? Whammo! Even though you don't yet own TiVo or a DVR, it has sauntered onto your Top 40 products list, simply because you're thinking about it, talking about it, and feel some passion for the concept of a better TV viewing experience.

We're exposed to thousands of products every day, and experience many more indirectly, so we're constantly bombarded with reasons to add or remove things from our list. Poor service at a Starbucks or an incredible display of lawnmowers at a Home Depot may be enough for some people, but for most it takes a significant experience with the product to get it on the list. The experience can be personal, like your first date at a restaurant with your future spouse, or more functional, like ordering a pair of shoes on Zappos and receiving your first overnight free delivery. Advertising can be a driver for the Top 40 list. Geico's talking lizard and amazing real customer/real celebrity commercials are certainly worth talking about (I like the one with Peter Frampton), and make great icebreakers for that tedious cocktail party.

Let's imagine for a moment that there is a fantastic Marketing Olympics, and it's held between the summer and winter games. (If you miss it, reruns would be shown after figure skating.) As a marketer, getting your product into the Top 40 would be medal-worthy, but it wouldn't be enough to get you the gold. That's reserved for the top three to five products, which are significantly more meaningful to people than those farther down, and thus get talked about considerably more than the rest.

Those pinnacle spots typically are connected in some way with the person's most intense passions and favorite hobbies. A base-ball fanatic, for example, will pay close attention to ads for sporting gear and engage in conversations about the ins and outs of Little League catchers' mitts. A music fanatic may actively seek out the latest release from a post-Weezer Rivers Cuomo (pre-Weezer's return, of course) and an auto enthusiast may pay attention to an eBay auction for a 1976 International Harvester.

But trends and fads also play a significant role. Even if you're not a technophile, you may have found yourself discussing the iPhone when it hit the market.

It's important to note that products may earn a spot on the Top 40 list, not because they are beloved, but rather, because they are reviled. The product that disappoints can just as easily end up on the list as the one that changes our lives for the better.

The good news (for those with bad products) is that the list is in a constant state of flux. Evolution proceeds very quickly in the product world. One day, the members of your parent group can talk about nothing else than video baby monitors. After you've bought one and the novelty of watching your baby crawl around her crib wears off, the product is rarely mentioned.

For marketers, the implications of the Top 40 list are huge. Accelerating and managing word of mouth is about figuring out how to crack the Top 40 for as many consumers as possible at once—and then staying there for as long as possible. Because the list is constantly changing, marketers need to implement programs that repeatedly offer reasons for people to think about a product and keep it on their list. The big bang of a PR hit, a big contest, or flashy advertising may get something onto someone's list for a moment, but in order to really harness word of mouth, the heavy lifting comes from multiple interactions over time that create a Top 40 word of mouth maintenance plan.

In the late 1960s, the cartoon *Scooby-Doo* began its own maintenance plan, which landed it in *The Guinness Book of World Records* for having produced the most episodes of any animated

TV series. Scooby is recognized so widely that it's no surprise *Animal Planet* named him one of the 50 Greatest TV Animals and *TV Guide* ranked him #22 on the 50 Greatest Cartoon Characters of All Time. In a twist of fate, it just so happens that the voice of Shaggy, Scooby's ever-confused sidekick, is none other than Casey Kasem.

If that isn't worth a marketing gold medal, I don't know what is.

3. Collective Shared Experiences

HAD HERBERT KRUGMAN been in charge, those incredibly annoying HeadOn commercials never would have seen the light of day.

And that would have been a damn shame.

If you've been living under a rock on Mars, and you haven't seen these particular commercials, they're the ones that repeat the phrase, "Apply Directly to Forehead" over and over, against the green-screen grid backdrop of actors swiping at their foreheads with the HeadOn headache remover. The narrator makes it sound as if enthusiastically applying gel to your forehead is as normal as fixing yourself a bowl of cereal.

Herbert Krugman, had he been in charge of the creative, never would have approved such a spot. When he was an employee at General Electric, Krugman wrote a paper titled, *The Impact of Television Advertising: Learning Without Involvement*, in which he argued that after three exposures to a commercial message, further repetitions have little effect. The first time you hear a message, you ask, "What is it?" The second time, you ask, "What of it?" The third time reminds you that you're already aware of the product. Everything after that is wasted. So, according to Krugman, you would only have to hear "Apply Directly to Forehead" three times before getting the point.

Most media planners know about Krugman and the term he coined, "effective frequency," which signifies the number of times a person must be exposed to an advertising message before it generates a response—and before the following exposures are essentially wasted. But there's an important footnote to Krugman's much-revered theory. He believed that there was some value in all that repetition because we don't actually forget anything we've seen on TV; we just put it aside until or unless we have a need. Then—and only then—do we respond to the repetition. In short, Krugman argued that getting people to become conscious of a product is easy; getting them to have a real need for it is another story altogether.

Creating that need is clearly no walk in the park. In today's marketplace, where a significant portion of advertising is seen as interruptive and lacking in credibility, generating demand is impossible without some form of consumer advocacy, whether it's an honest testimonial written on a retailer's website or the recommendation from a neighbor. As a result, the concept of effective frequency has to be rethought. In every marketing medium, the focus is shifting away from mindless repetition and toward meaningful engagement.

So why, in this age of anti-repetition, do these throwback commercials for HeadOn actually work? Because they create something entirely new and relevant to current trends: the collective shared experience. People love to share their reaction—part disgust, part anger, part amusement—to the HeadOn commercials. They want to recount the experience of hearing it for the first time and commiserate about the tenth time they heard it when they stubbed their toe sprinting for the remote control to mute the sound when the commercial came on. Whether someone shut it off or turned it up, it gave people something to talk about and a reason to feel connected to each other. This kind of connection, a collective shared experience, can fill the marketing crater left by the decline of effective frequency.

Each of us has been a member of a group of some kind, like the chess club you've been sharing end-game, king-safety, and pawn-structure strategies with for the last decade, or the ad hoc bunch of co-workers you eat lunch with every day. Generating collective shared experiences around brands and products has the same characteristics as any other group experience—it brings a sense of being chosen, belonging, and becoming part of an inner circle, as opposed to suffering as the outsider looking in.

The collective shared experience of those who were driven crazy by HeadOn commercials was derived from the mutual acknowledgment of having seen the commercial and reacting to it. This type of experience is hardly a deep, long-lasting, or even very positive one—but it does show that brands can cause groups to form around all kinds of experiences.

Citibank and American Express, for example, have partnered to create a private cardholder community. The benefits of belonging go far beyond lower rates and reduced fees; it's about becoming a member of an exclusive customer service group, with access to private jet service, dining reservations, and indulgent experiences like golfing at the world-famous St. Andrews course or enjoying the services of a private chef. Yes, the offering is basically a credit card, but it's a collective experience that only a few are invited to share. Gaining admission to this club is only the beginning. Members get early invitations to various events and offerings, and being among the very first to take part can heighten the experience even more. With every early notification, additional nugget of knowledge, or peek-around-the-corner, the collective shared experience only gets stronger.

But the most critical component of generating the bond of a collective shared experience is providing a product experience that will provoke people to talk with one another. The more monumental the experience, the greater the likelihood that people will go out of their way to tell others about it.

Volkswagen provided an opportunity for 1,500 of its Alpha Driver's Club members to take a private test drive of the new Passat—before it was released to market, mind you. It wasn't just getting in on the action early that mattered most. It was that Alpha Drivers who opted in could have the vehicle delivered to their home and have it all to themselves for 48 hours of driving with family and friends, showing off, and talking it up. Those who took part posted photos and engaged in conversation on consumer-run VW community sites. They were also allowed a $1,000 rebate for a limited period, which enabled VW to track those sales that came about as the result of the experience—nearly $9 million worth.

The VW collective experience was pretty far up on the word of mouth generation scale, but humbler ones can also bring people together and get them talking. When people receive a brand-new, no-obligation, whatever-it-is in the mail—even if it's just a trio of Wisp Air Fresheners, a package of Hillshire Farm Deli Meats, or a spanking new Sonicare Toothbrush and UV Sanitizer—they feel part of a group that engenders some measure of loyalty. Getting the package is a much more significant experience than merely receiving a coupon for the same product. The recipient may well redeem the coupon, but it's unlikely she'll talk much about the "experience," because it hardly qualifies as one. And forget about sending along an informational packet. That's a leftover from the direct mail era and could be considered an anti-experience, one that few will want to talk about.

If you're seeking to motivate consumers to actively talk about your products with others, you need to consider every element of their interaction with you, and make it special. Private invitations, classified knowledge, and special experiences all add up, with the result that people feel that they are part of a collective shared experience. Anything short of that—any corner-cutting—limits the consumer from generating the perfect thimbleful of effective frequency.

Apply that directly to your forehead, if you need to remember it.

4. The Post-Purchase Effect

ON JUNE 29, 2007, the long wait for the iPhone came to an end.

Just five months earlier, in typically grand style, Steve Jobs had announced the new iPhone at the Macworld Expo. Almost immediately, speculation began about every aspect of the beautiful gadget: how it would change mobile media forever, and which features and functions might be included. Some 40 major publications printed articles about the announcement, and the flood of press attention continued until it swelled into an absolute frenzy a month before the release date.

Everyone had an opinion about every aspect of the phone, and people took up sides: those who planned to buy the iPhone and those who were going to shun it. People debated the price point (too high?) and analyzed Apple's partnership with AT&T, the company that outmaneuvered the sluggish Verizon to close the deal. Bloggers blogged furiously. Consumers were dying to start consuming.

In those five months, Jobs created a "triangle of urgency." First, the product had the broad and immediate appeal of a new mobile phone. Second, Jobs added a tantalizing dash of exclusivity by setting the price high and hinting that not everyone was really worthy of his new creation. And third, he created an air of mystery. Jobs did not reveal everything about the phone and released only

20 units before the launch. In short, he managed the medium of word of mouth to near perfection.

Marketers will be studying Apple's word of mouth playbook for years to come: the timing of the press announcements; the sequence in which they released ads and the amount of time between them; the words they used and the fonts they flaunted; how they hired models whose hands were large enough to make the relatively hunky iPhone look smaller. All of the careful planning and thoughtful management of anticipation didn't go unnoticed. Hundreds of people waited in line for days, hoping to be among the first to get their ordinary-sized hands on one. Apple had masterfully manipulated the public's eagerness for a massive transformation of the mobile phone category, and the lead-up to the product's release was pulled off without a hitch.

But to truly understand the medium of word of mouth, you have to consider what happened *after* the release, when Jobs and his team handed the baton to the consumers. They exhibited a pattern of post-purchase behavior that produced word of mouth in its most credible and effective form.

That's when things really took off.

On June 30, 2007, the day after the official release of the iPhone, the chatter grew louder, the speculation grew even more intense, and people discussed every tiny component of the device. The site www.anandtech.com dissected it, examining and analyzing every scrap of injection-molded plastic, colored wire, and the sandwich of paper-thin layers that compose the innovative touch screen.

Ordinary consumers evaluated and speculated and moaned. Some complained that their Shure headphones didn't fit right. Others suspected that Apple's exclusion of a standard "cut and paste" clipboard wasn't an oversight, but a deliberate choice made to maximize processing speed. One creative individual figured out how to reconfigure the phone's components to make a microscope.

Within a day or two, iPhones began showing up in schools and offices, homes, and health clubs. New owners could not wait to show off their toy. They'd corner friends and colleagues and urge them to check out the phone, touch it. Onlookers ooh-ed and ahh-ed when the iPhone possessor finger-motioned an image, causing it to swell, and then swiped in the other direction, making it contract. In offices, little groups clustered in hallways, distracted by the lucky few who had somehow gotten their hands on the new Apple miracle. I wandered into a conference room and a dozen people looked up guiltily, as if they'd been caught surfing porn on the Internet; as they dispersed, the owner hastily pocketed his new treasure and escaped quickly without making eye contact.

The action went on for weeks. Those who had gotten their hands on an iPhone constantly showed it off to anyone and everyone around them. This wasn't just your ordinary show-and-tell, conducted with the intention of impressing and inspiring others. Rather, it was driven by an urgent subconscious need to receive validation. The owners wanted to be reassured that they had done a smart thing, the right thing, a justifiable thing. And it's this behavior that is perhaps the most powerful driver of effective word of mouth.

These early iPhone buyers were experiencing a particularly acute instance of the post-purchase effect: that many of us spread the majority of word of mouth about a product or service just *after* we've completed a purchase. Once we've plunked down our cash, it's as if a switch has been flipped. We've come to a conclusion, made a bet, and feel compelled to become highly vocal advocates of the wisdom of our gamble.

The good news: In this post-purchase window, the new product is guaranteed to be high on the consumer's Top 40 list. No matter how much word of mouth they might have engaged in before the product release, and prior to purchase, it rarely has the conviction and urgency that post-purchase word of mouth often has.

There are three main reasons why this occurs.

- **POST-PURCHASE IS THE BEST TIME TO SHARE** because other people are highly aware of the product and most receptive to discussions about it. There is a natural curiosity for new products and experiences, and often there is a timely relevance. If I bought an iPhone six months after it was released and whipped it out in a meeting expecting to drum up a lively discussion, I'd be out of luck.

- **THIRD-PERSON ACCOUNTS BECOME FIRST-PERSON NARRATIVES.** Pre-purchase, we've spent a significant amount of time asking others what they'd recommend, researching online or in-store, and paying particular attention to television, print, and radio advertisements. All our dialogues are based on the stories we've heard from or about others. The pre-purchase discussion about which GPS system to buy is far less informative or convincing than the story about how your wife almost flipped her lid when she heard Dumbledore's voice telling her to take a left turn. First-hand stories are infinitely more influential than third-party recommendations.

- Most important, **WE SEEK VALIDATION FROM OTHERS.** We want people around us to say that our decision makes sense and that they might have done (or will do) the same thing. We want to believe that we are smart consumers and are mighty skillful at sifting through piles of data and forming coherent opinions. Without realizing it, we proactively approach others and talk to them in a way that suggests they should consider purchasing themselves.

We forcefully argue that the new product has brought value to our lives and learn how to override any objections we might hear. It's as if we are salespeople ourselves, convincing and challenging others, seeking to bring them around to our point of view.

The post-purchase effect can last a few days, weeks, or months, depending on the size of the investment the individual has made and the particular character of the product. No matter how long it lasts, this is a unique and incredible moment in a product's life cycle. One in which consumers feel absolutely compelled to make believers of the people around them. Word of mouth skills go into overdrive. We practice our most persuasive techniques. We extol our knowledge to accelerate the decisions of others.

As for the iPhone, Apple generated more than its fair share of persuasion, with the post-purchase effect in full force for weeks after the introduction. But during the 10th week, Jobs and team did something highly unexpected and irregular—they cut the retail price of the iPhone from $599 to $399, a massive reduction so early in the game.

Many who had purchased the iPhone at the higher price felt slightly burned. They'd spent weeks showing and sharing and telling others why they were so smart to hop on the bandwagon of this premium, only-for-the-few product. Now their peers could follow their lead, but looked much smarter because they had waited a few weeks and been financially rewarded for doing so. Although Apple later offered a rebate to early purchasers, the damage had been done. As effectively as they'd begun the post-purchase word of mouth, they just as convincingly stopped it in its tracks. For weeks after, few were eager to reveal that they had been early iPhone adopters. The discussion shifted from the product itself to the rather uncomfortable and even embarrassing subject of whether or not the owner had received a rebate.

Who really wants to talk about that?

5. The Comparative Value of Word of Mouth

THERE'S NO QUESTION that word of mouth is one of the most powerful marketing mediums on the planet.

For years, various studies and statistics have quantified the phenomenon and proved that the recommendation of a friend, family member, acquaintance—or even a stranger—is a primary driver of most purchase decisions.

Today, marketers can deploy word of mouth programs that are coordinated, manageable, and measurable—applying such standardized marketing techniques as pre-purchase analysis or purchase intent variations to determine value. New metrics systems such as Net Promoter® Scoring, a method of analyzing the percentage of people who recommend a product in contrast to those who disparage it, help marketers understand the value of their word of mouth initiatives.

As a new and "unproven" medium, organized word of mouth activity is often held to a higher standard than traditional counterparts like TV or radio advertising. As a result, marketers have spent a lot of time trying to prove that word of mouth really drives sales and developing ways to measure the return on investment (ROI) of their word of mouth initiatives. It's no wonder they do. Most marketers have to prove it to their CMO.

But what has plenty of marketers in traction is trying to understand the value of their word of mouth spending in comparison with the dollars they've been spending on the other marketing media that have been dominant in the last 50 years.

What exactly is a word of mouth conversation worth, in comparison with a traditional impression?

There are many theories. One research study in the United Kingdom suggests that a word of mouth dialogue is 1,000 times more powerful than a standard ad impression, a number that is likely as fantastical as it is large. Others, such as public relations master Jack Trout, argue that word of mouth may be "overhyped" and limited in its ability to drive much more return than standard communications methods (the ones that he, not coincidentally, happens to deploy).

Theorists abound; marketers demand to know the answer before they spend a single penny on this activity. So, the Dude abides.* Studies are funded, papers are written, and ideas are romanticized. Procter & Gamble teamed up with Nielsen, the measurement gurus, to fund Project Apollo, a semi-secret initiative that aimed to track every moment that a consumer "engaged" with the brand—from first exposure to a bit of marketing to purchase. Each engagement would be noted, given a value, and linked to the resulting purchase. It's about as easy as it sounds.

* What's a book without a *Big Lebowski* reference?

The intensity of the efforts to come up with a formula for measuring word of mouth is evidence of the power of the medium, but it's going to take years for people to align on the best equation. Or maybe it will never happen; there is no such equation for traditional advertising, after all.

But for those of you who don't want to wait, let me provide a neat little shortcut:

(# of Traditional Media Impressions) × (Average Length of Impression) = (# of Word of Mouth Communications) × (Average Length of Word of Mouth Communication)

Want to compare a word of mouth spend to the cost of a 30-second TV spot? Here you go:

Average word of mouth communication = 8 minutes (480 seconds)
Length of TV commercial = 30 seconds

Let's say a marketer buys 300 showings of the commercial on programs that typically attract 200,000 viewers. That's 60,000,000 impressions (assume for a moment that they do get that many viewers and all of those viewers actually watch the commercial.) The equation is:

(60,000,000 TV Impressions) × (30 seconds) = (# of Word of Mouth Communications) × (480 seconds).

So, if you do the math and solve for #, to generate an impact equal to 60 million television impressions, you'd need only 3.75 million word of mouth communications. The same formula could be run for just about any medium available.

But, although this calculation usually provides some comfort to marketers who need to justify their budgets, it is merely a quantitative measure. The dialogue involved in a word of mouth consumer conversation creates much greater value than does the passive experience of watching a 30-second commercial, no matter how clever it might be. We all know in our bones that the power of a recommendation—an opinion being delivered from one consumer to another—is enormous. It's just that no one has figured out exactly how to put a numerical value on it.

I've heard that the person who does will get a comet named after him.

6. Word of Mouth Goes Global

IMAGINE YOU'RE IN THE CHECKOUT LINE of a supermarket in Dublin, Ireland.

You're new to the city and are still finding your way around, so you ask the cashier if he knows where the nearest gas station is. Unfortunately, even though he's Irish, he's new to Dublin, just started working at the store, and doesn't have any idea. As you make small talk about what it's like living in such an exciting place, you realize that the line of people behind you, locals shopping for their groceries, must have overheard your conversation and your request for directions, yet not a single one of them offered to point you in the right direction.

You shouldn't be surprised. According to an ex-pat friend of mine who lived in Dublin for eight years, the Irish would consider it rude to enter into a dialogue without being directly addressed; social norms would label that as being nosy or just plain rude: If you're not asked directly, it's not your conversation. Rather than being considered a helpful stranger—as you might be in America— you would be thought of as intrusive. Social norms and friendliness aside, this provides a startling insight for marketers in that culture: Word of mouth just wouldn't work as effectively.

While I've heard other Irish natives discount this theory

completely—of course we're friendly!—the consideration is an important one. Although word of mouth might be the fastest growing alternative media form in the United States, other cultures may realize a different growth path or trend. Not because of a lack of interest or value in people making recommendations to each other, but because people share information differently across different cultures.

Yet, over the last few years, coordinated word of mouth networks have popped up all over the globe. The Nordic countries are home to one of the fastest growing communities, called Buzzador, which at last count boasted nearly 100,000 volunteers throughout Sweden, Denmark, and Finland. Azoomba, hailing from South Korea, possesses a network of millions of moms who take part in digital word of mouth programs; Turkey's FikriMühim has become one of the first new media strategies that marketers in that country have the ability to deploy; and then there are the secretive folks in Russia who are developing a new type of word of mouth initiative, but they refuse to talk with anyone about it. (Irony rears its ugly head!)

The British have a very particular view on the efficacy of word of mouth. Many locals believe it has worked in America because we're appreciative of others' opinions, but believe that it wouldn't work in the United Kingdom because people are just too cynical there. According to one outspoken Brit (who spoke only on the guarantee of anonymity), "We like to think we're cynical, but it's just how we hide the fact that we're sweet."

The real issue for most people in the British culture—not unlike many in the rest of the world—is that they feel they can't trust marketers. But once you clarify that word of mouth isn't about cornering your mate in a pub to sneakily talk about your favorite chocolates or what gadget you shaved with that morning, the cynicism melts away and the sweetness emerges. Brits are just as receptive as, if not more so than, people in other cultures.

Canadians are not particularly doubtful about how effective word of mouth might be in their country, in general, but they do have a specific concern. They worry that, because the Canadian population is so concentrated in a few key urban hubs—Toronto, Ottawa, Montreal, Vancouver, and Edmonton—with the rest of the country characterized by vast open spaces inhabited only by land barons and herds of elk, word of mouth will be unable to proliferate. I say not to worry, the vast distance between neighbors in some parts of Canada actually helps the spread of word of mouth, as information becomes all that much more valuable.

Regardless of location or cultural norms, the evidence points to the fact that our word of mouth behaviors across continents are more similar than they are different. In October 2007, in a classroom in the heart of Berlin, 15 people representing 15 different global word of mouth organizations got together to discuss the evolution of word of mouth philosophy across the globe. In many ways, except for accents, fashion statements, and culinary preferences, it was almost impossible to tell one organization from another.

The global landscape for word of mouth is just beginning to take shape. The idea of one person talking to another knows few boundaries—regardless of how far apart you live or what your main choice of communication happens to be. In Japan, it's alleged that word of mouth will occur more often on mobile phones than it will across the Internet. In Italy, the groups that engage in word of mouth seem to be much larger than in most other Western societies.

The truth is hard to avoid: No matter where we live or what our cultural disposition, the opinions we generate are the bonds that link us all.

With that, I say *auf wiedersehen*, and *hâo yùn*.

II. WHAT YOU PROBABLY KNOW ALREADY

(UNLESS YOU DON'T)

According to their parents,

"gifted" children possess characteristics that dramatically set them apart from other children. Moms and dads of precocious preschoolers explain that their special child learns faster and more deeply than the other little rugrats in class. They will gush (and gush and gush) about their kid's benchmark-setting skills in finger painting and their NEA-boggling ability to recite the alphabet forward, backward, and in pig Latin.

It turns out that gifted children typically have an unquenchable desire to understand the world. They ask endless questions about everything and anything. They love to challenge their parents, debate their teachers, and show up their friends.

I was not one of those children. Perhaps you were not, either.

But fret not. In some sort of cosmic payback for their overly cognitive psyche, it's not unheard of for gifted children to obsessively and repeatedly get mentally stuck asking the same questions over and over and over.

1. Some People Just Want to Hate Word of Mouth

HERE'S AN ABSURD REAL-LIFE MOMENT that I actually endured. I was describing our word of mouth network and passionate consumers to a marketing director for a huge fragrance company. She listened not very patiently and then interrupted me. "I can't remember any time that I offered or received an opinion about a product or service to or from any other person. Ever. In my life." She glared at me.

I shifted my weight from one butt cheek to the other. I felt a gurgling in my throat. "You never recommended a restaurant to someb. . . ."

"Never," she said.

"Or mentioned, let's say, the name of a clothing shop wh. . . ."

"Not once," she said.

"Or brought up one of your brand. . . ."

"NO!"

The alleged conversation had come to an end. I packed up my ideas and scurried away.

Some people, many of them gifted marketers, go purple with rage at the idea of organized word of mouth. They see it as some convoluted con game in which the mark is your bosom buddy or sainted granny. When we started BzzAgent, I received lots of anonymous email. "What you're doing is quite close to slavery," one person wrote. Another cussed me out and referenced George Orwell's *1984*.

Such rage is fueled by fear. Word of mouth will devour the final tiny crumb of trust we have in our society. It will turn people into robotic drones, remotely controlled by immoral marketers. It will destroy relationships and wreck homes. People will sell their souls for a chance to sample a greaseless surface cleanser or taste a particularly stinky type of cheese.

I smell irony.

Marketers denouncing a con game? Marketers who have spent zillions of dollars and the best years of their lives devising ways to deliver exaggerations and tell outright lies. Paying gobs of cash to some attractive Aussie actress to smooch a Spanish guy in the rain on a rooftop for one commercial intended to create a lasting brand image. To them, a word of mouth network is an abomination, a perversion of the natural order of things?

Let me offer just a few examples of real marketing perversions:

- THE LEANER, who poses as a product advocate, but really couldn't care less. Often seen at bars, loudly ordering brand-name beverages.
- THE PHONY TOURIST, who asks real people to take his picture with a cell phone camera, making sure to mention the brand name.

- **STREET TEAMS,** who create trumped-up scenes that disrupt the flow of real city life.
- **GUERILLA MARKETERS,** who think of marketing as a kind of warfare, with sorties carried out against unsuspecting citizens.
- **AND OTHERS,** who are so sneaky and underhanded they don't even have names.

Many of us have bought into these activities at one time or another, believed the actors, been intrigued by the product, and hastened ourselves to Target to fill our cart to the brim, only to discover later that we've been had. That is when purple rage is truly justified.

In *The Truman Show*, Jim Carrey's character is living his life in a TV show, but he doesn't know it. Everything that happens is controlled by the network. Everything he sees is actually a stage set. All the people he interacts with are members of the Screen Actors Guild.

The movie resonated because it sometimes seems that our lives are truly like that. Only it's not the network that controls who we are and what we do, it's those indefatigable marketers. No matter how sophisticated we become at catching on to their tricks, they're often just a step or two ahead of us. It's hard not to get fooled, to be swayed, even when we know it's all baloney.

But maybe 20th-century marketing was an anomaly, just a

short blip during which educated people gave in to some strange weakness for snappy tag lines, happy family TV kitchens, celebrity endorsers, animatronic bunnies, and product placements. Maybe this new phase of word of mouth media is really nothing more than the future form of the buying process of the past, when a person's best way of learning about a product or service was from the recommendation (or warning) of a trusted friend or cowhand.

The difference is that today word of mouth marketing isn't so random; it has some shape and process. Even so, the talkers behave pretty much as they did in the old days. They don't punch a time card. They don't follow a marketer's script. They talk about the good, the bad, the beautiful, and the ugly aspects of the product. They talk when they want and how they want. They don't have to talk at all if they don't feel like it.

As a result, the emerging word of mouth phenomenon produces incredibly rich and authentic conversations. Conversations that matter to others, that help them make decisions about what is really worth buying. It may be more accelerated than the word of mouth of old, but it's still full of the authenticity that makes it so powerful.

Yet somehow this hatred for the deceptive practices of marketers was transferred to the ability to tap into the honest dialogue of real consumers.

So if you spend your days fighting word of mouth, pretending that it's some new reprehensible burden on your otherwise marketing-free world, it might be time to give up that misconception. You want a better way for marketers to deal with consumers? You have it. It's right in front of you, and it's not demonizing the planet.

That actress probably doesn't even wear high-priced perfume anyway.

2. How to Get Hundreds of Thousands of People to "Work" for Free

HERE'S A FARFETCHED IDEA worth pondering: a transportable time card (TTC). What is it? It tracks everything you do, everything you say, everywhere you go, everyone you meet, every second of every day. You wear it around your wrist. Each citizen is provided with his or her very own card at birth, with some cryptic number like 66bob*!A.

The TTC transmits your data to the much-dreaded Bureau of Behavior Management (BBM) for analysis. Call up a friend to schedule a lunch, and your TTC automatically notes the 15 seconds consumed by the task. Complain to a co-worker about your boss's habit of taking everyone else's ideas for his own, and the tiny click and whir you hear on your wrist signals that your 20 minutes of gripe time have been reported.

You receive gold stars for the positive things you do. Redeemable for things you need, like virgin fig vinegar and hand soap, and things you want, like (if it were me) tiny marshmallows. You get red Xs for your negative actions. If you accumulate too many of them, you are punished in some way that you, in particular, really dislike. For me, that would be going to bed on an empty stomach.

Here's another ridiculous idea that many smart people have stuck in their heads. Word of mouth advocates are *working* when they share an opinion about a product or service with their friends, colleagues, neighbors, co-workers, or kindergarten teachers.

Yes, alert and knowledgeable people actually publicly state that they believe this.

Why is this ridiculous? Because we know that people naturally and consistently talk about products and services as a part of their conversations with one another. In fact, research shows that about 15 percent of our daily conversations have some product- or service-related content.

Even if those alert and knowledgeable people accept this distinction, they part company with me when we come to the "managed" part—that is, when opinion sharing about products and services takes place because of participation in a reasonably well-defined and coordinated word of mouth network. Then, they argue, natural sharing is transformed into nefarious talk-for-hire.

I say that it's the natural (and positive) evolution of the conundrum that is marketing. For about 40 years or so, we all kind of went along with the game. Ads could be pretty amusing, after all. And the act of buying was just a part of life—sometimes fun, sometimes not. Marketing became a technique of interruptive savvy. Marketers spent billions of dollars to make people aware of their products and, by God, buy them in large quantities. The goal was simple: Convert the ordinary human being into a consumption machine.

But gradually, people began to resent the terrific glut of bad marketing and reject the idea that marketers should decide what products and services should thrive and which should die.

So consumers began to turn the tables on marketers. They learned to evaluate claims and ignore promotions and see through clever slogans. "Just Do It" sounded good when Bo Jackson was doing the doing, but the rest of us weren't nearly as motivated. Few checked if their coffee was "Good to the Last Drop"; they wanted to taste for themselves what was worth drinking. Today, as a result, the marketer of a new credit card needs to spend twice what was necessary 10 years ago and captures only half as many consumers.

The marketer now faces a dilemma expressed in a bizarre inverse equation of marketing: *Marketers are spending more and more money delivering messages that consumers are trying harder and harder to avoid.*

And yet, that does not mean that people have totally rejected marketing messages. To the contrary, it's the way those marketing messages are delivered that has created the problem, it's not that marketing itself is bad. There is (at least) one place where product and service messages are not only welcomed but actively embraced: a word of mouth network. Here people do things that look a lot like traditional marketing activities. They:

- Help others become aware of new products.

- Dole out coupons to friends.
- Email the URL of company websites to their moms.
- Share samples with co-workers.
- Talk about product features and benefits.
- Tell the manufacturer (not to mention friends!) what they don't like about a product.

They are in essence marketing products, but without looking like marketers, talking like marketers, acting like marketers, or most important, *thinking* like marketers. They don't get paid for what they do. And they're not trying to transform their pals and peers into consumption machines.

What gives?

The characteristics of a word of mouth network make consumers comfortable in engaging about products: They don't feel like targets, part of the equation, numbers on a spreadsheet, or that their eyeballs are more important than their hearts or brains. The network treats them as they would be treated by friends. The brand respects them and says, in effect, that it would like to spend some time with them. People are given the opportunity to make their own choices, rather than being told what to choose. As a result, they want to stick with the brand and are willing to give back to it in spades.

So where does this leave us?

Participants look like they work for free because they're not actually working at all.

3. Samples That Count

LET'S SAY YOU'RE A BASEBALL FANATIC. You're given the opportunity to bat in a major league baseball game at Fenway Park. You step up to the plate. You gaze out over the stands, at the 33,423 people watching you. Your mom and dad are sitting on the edge of their seats in the owner's box.

The pitcher goes into his wind-up. The ball comes zipping at you, a 96-mph fastball that looks like it might break just when it reaches the plate. You wonder, "Maybe I should bunt?" Then you think about all those high school classmates who said, "He'll never amount to much." You decide to take your best swing. Go for the hit that could turn into a run and win the game.

The crowd stands, cheering wildly, of course.

Here's the rough equivalent of a bunt in marketing: giving away a free sample. It may get your product to first base, but that's about it. People like free samples, but it doesn't mean very much or lead to much of anything unless it creates conversations and furthers interactions.

Here's another way to think about it.

You're 22 years old. It's spring break in, let's say, Cancun. You're hot. Not warm, as in temperature, mind you. Actually sexy. Damn, you look good. Scantily clad in an itsy-bitsy ensemble, showing off your six-pack abs, grooving to MTV-style rhythms at the bar.

A guy comes up to you, wearing T-shirt and surfer shorts emblazoned all over with the logo of a sunscreen brand, and offers a sample-size tube of SPF-8 (you still don't completely believe there's a link between UV rays and skin cancer) containing thiotaurine and essence of jojoba, plus that taurine stuff they have in Red Bull (for marketing cred and hipness).

"Try it," he says. Suddenly remembering the nasty sunburn you got last year when you fell asleep by the pool, you accept his offer and slather on the goo. The guy moves on to the next overexposed partier, like a happy-go-lucky wolf looking for more sheep. He has a quota, of course, so no time to waste.

What is the result of this random product encounter? Trial, which is important, but the long-term impact is suspect. You might like the stuff enough that you'll look for, or at least recognize, the brand next time you go shopping for a sunscreen. Here's what you almost certainly won't do: Dash over to the rest of your super-hot clan and say, "Hey, check out this really great sunscreen. It's got featerone and hohoja!"

What makes a sample more than a sample?

- **HOW IT'S DELIVERED.** Rather than getting a product shoved in your hand by some nameless wastrel wandering up to you with intent to unload, you receive a nice package in the mail. Lots of information. Maybe a DVD. Perhaps a hat with a sun-protective brim with no logo; something you might actually wear.

- **WHEN IT'S DELIVERED.** Marketers connive to deliver a sample at a moment of critical need: sunscreen at the beach, antacid at the ballpark. But people rarely form coherent opinions at times like those. Suppose you had received the sample well *before* you left for Cancun. You tried it. You bought a bigger jug. You packed it carefully. You had it with you on the beach with your friends, before you hit the bar. Sampling forces you to respond on the fly at an unexpected moment, to look into the product's eyes and suddenly fall in love, but that's just not how things actually work. You need to learn about products on your own time, in your own way.

- **THE NATURE OF THE DIALOGUE THAT SURROUNDS IT.** People don't long to become a sampling mechanism any more than they wish to be a consumption machine. They want to be thought of as a brand evaluator, a channel for information. They want to speak in their own voice about the product, and get a response when they do. They want a dialogue, not a diatribe.

So let's say all of these wonderful sampling things happened to you. One year later. You're 23. On spring break. (You're on the five-year graduation plan.) You believe the brand values your opinion, thinks of you as important. You don't hesitate to share your opinion about it with others. About the risks of too much sun. How this goo really doesn't dissolve in the water. How handy the tube is. Where you can buy the stuff. The purpose of thiotaurine. The glory of jojoba.

You're so knowledgeable and enthusiastic that one of your buddies asks, "What, are you getting paid?"

You're a little offended by the question. "Of course not. This is really good stuff," you say.

For a moment, your caffeinated sunscreen seems like more of a friend than the friend does.

4. Lying Is for Liars

IN EARLY 2007, a baggage handler named Robert Lewis was sorting through some stray luggage at the lost and found area of Kansas City International Airport. He grabbed the handle of an oversized bag and found it was too heavy to lift. The bag had no identification, so he unzipped it and took a peek inside. Staring back at him was a stash of jewelry and precious stones.

At that time, Lewis didn't know that the haul was worth about $266,000, but it was obvious that what was in the bag was valuable. One stone could probably have covered his mortgage payments for a year. Without a moment's hesitation, Lewis zipped up the bag and went to investigate. He discovered that the bag had accidentally "fallen off" the back of a Brink's security truck and that it belonged to Helzberg Diamonds, a company that owns a chain of jewelry stores. Lewis did the right thing: He returned the bag to its rightful owners and, as a thank you for his good will, they cut him a check for $10,000.

Robert Lewis isn't alone: Regardless of what we see on the 6 P.M. news (or, more likely, www.cnn.com), most people generally do the right and honorable thing, even when it might be easy to do otherwise.

When we started BzzAgent (which, if you haven't gathered by

now, is a word of mouth media company), it didn't even cross our minds that people would want to take advantage of our system. Maybe I was too trusting, overly passionate, or just plain too naïve to think that people would lie to get the ability to try products and services, no strings attached.

Other people, however, have been only too quick to assume that our system must be a breeding ground for deception, and the prime suspect for them is the reports that people in our network write about their product-related conversations. In 2007, nearly 15,000 people took the time each week to document their word of mouth interactions about some product or other. The report might relate how the correspondent shared her butter spread or insect repellant and the influence—or lack thereof—that it had. Or it could detail the pride the reporter felt when his knowledge about coffee roasting impressed his date or how a TV ad started a conversation about a pair of shoes that the volunteer had received from us.

But why would they bother doing that?

Whatever the content, something about these reports brings out the skeptics. When I describe the reporting process in a meeting or speech, someone inevitably pipes up, voice rising with indignation and disgust, and shrieks, "How can you be sure these people aren't lying?"

It's unfortunate that we're predisposed in today's world to distrust those around us, to assume that, if the rules can be bent, someone will get right to it. We seem to tolerate minor acts of dishonesty such as taking a few extra candies from the mint jar at the front of a restaurant or temporarily disabling a parking meter by slipping a tiny piece of paper in the coin slot. Whatever the reason, there's no getting around the fact that some just expect others to err on the side of "getting away with it" if at all possible.

When it comes to word of mouth, there are two dominant perspectives. Some argue that deception must be rampant given that this is a trust-based system. Others believe that people, in general, are good, and will do good if given the choice. (For you believers in do-gooders, the next section could be skipped. Take a break, eat a snack, watch some TV, pet your cat. For those who like to take pencils, pads of paper, a stapler, and a few ink cartridges from your office supply cabinet for home use, this little bit is mainly for you.)

To the people who see deception everywhere, let me offer the following arguments:

- **THE PROCESS OF JOINING A WORD OF MOUTH NETWORK WEEDS OUT MOST LIARS.** It takes a bit of work to get involved in a system like ours. You have to sign up, fill out a profile, do some training exercises, and then wait to be offered a campaign to join. When one becomes available, you have to read about it, answer some questions, wait to receive the product, learn about what the marketer is trying to accomplish, talk to your friends and family and, ultimately, file an actual report. This may not seem like a great deal of effort to those of you who are good-hearted, upstanding citizens, but to a system gamer it sounds like two years busting rock.

- **REPORT WRITING FILTERS OUT MOST OF THE NASTIES.** Let's assume, however, that there are some Navy Seal–level freebie hunters out there who are willing to put in the time necessary to join up and do, in fact, land a campaign and nab the product. But report writing? This is not the natural activity of the cyber-charlatan. True, you don't have to write a report to remain in the community. However, we're watching who does and who doesn't. If you never write a report it's unlikely you'll be offered another chance to participate. You may get a free pass once, but then the joyride ends.

- **THOSE WHO DO FILE REPORTS GET THEM WRONG.** OK, some of these Bruce Willis–like freebie hunters will grit their teeth and follow the rules in hopes of snatching up as much free stuff as possible. They're smart enough to realize that writing a report is the key to long-term success and it's worth the effort.

At this point, you can almost hear the naysayers let out a half-crazed chuckle. How hard can it be to make up a report? A couple of lines are all that's required, after all, and nobody's going to actually check the facts, are they?

Well, it's harder than you think. We have a small army of

people in our Communications Development Group (Com Dev) who really and truly read every report that comes in. They have collectively read more than 1 million reports since 2001. They're to organic word of mouth what Luke Skywalker is to the Force. They're bloodhounds running downwind and can sniff out deception from the tiniest of clues.

- **THOSE WHO WRITE GOOD REPORTS BECOME CONVERTS.** So now we're left with a tiny handful of determined deceivers. They realize that to really nail us, to savagely loot the system, they're going to have to fool us completely. They'll have to write a report absolutely chock-full of honesty and word of mouth goodness.

How will they accomplish this? They'll have to do what the real people do. Read all the information we send them. Experience the product as we suggest. Maybe even talk about it with others. Then sit down and pound out a report that is the word of mouth equivalent of *The Sun Also Rises.* To do so, they'll have to think hard about the product and how and where they might share their opinion about it.

Such a report can sometimes fool even the most experienced Com Dev.

Damn. They snared us. . . .

But. . . .

We really don't care.

You see, by the time these intelligently deceptive system swindlers have written their word of mouth opus, we've already captured them. By taking the time to join, putting in the effort to learn about the product, and applying the energy to write a believable story, they are already far more engaged with the product than they would be if they had been surrounded by even the slickest of multi-million-dollar marketing campaigns.

One last thing.

Word of mouth is as much about being conscious of a product as it is about the willingness to share opinions about it. Even would-be fraudsters can't avoid having learned a lot about a product, and somewhere, sometime, the product in question will get brought up in a conversation; or Jimmy Kimmel will mention it on his show; or a 30-second spot for it will air during *America's Funniest Home Videos* (don't laugh, it's the longest running show on TV); or they'll see it lying on someone's desk, and that knowledge will spill out and be listened to by others.

Yes, of course, we only want the contributions of honest word of mouth participants.

But, despite themselves, even those dishonest b@#*!s are creating valuable word of mouth. It's enough to make a liar blush.

5. Communications Can't Be Automated

THE FIRST TIME we went looking for money to fund BzzAgent was in 2001, when we were just a few guys with an idea. The investors we approached thought the idea of a word of mouth company was just plain silly. Two hundred investment groups passed on the concept of organized word of mouth. Go figure.

So, like any self-confident presidential candidate, we self-funded the company and found a cute and determined bee that we could use as our logo.

The second time we went looking for money, we knew the concept was working and had plenty of data to prove it. We began visiting wealthy individuals, sympathetic friends, and any family member who would listen to our story. We projected the pie charts, laid on the sweet talk, painted visions of the enormous scale we would achieve, and answered every question as if we actually knew what we were talking about.

Once again, some people said, "Nuh-uh." They didn't think this had a chance of becoming their country club investment (that is, the one they like to talk about when they go to their country club, 'cause it makes them sound ultracool. As in, "I just bought into a private island/movie production studio/Qi Gong academy with Richard Branson and Po Bronson.")

One of the major hurdles to becoming flush with cash was something you might not expect: the Com Dev part of the process. And it wasn't the potential for lying that caused the investors to chew ice from their drinks and gaze out the window. Many proffered the suggestion that there are technologies available that would enable us to automate the process and get the same result, and thus increase our margins and reduce the complexity of the business. Without automation, they made the assumption that the business would get bogged down with too much hands-on involvement.

Sometimes I get a bit worked up when I'm confronted with harebrained perspectives from gifted people, and this was one of those times. "It just so happens," I would say, "that Communications Development is one of the most important assets of our business. Automating it would be akin to telling a NASCAR driver that he isn't allowed to shift out of second gear."

Com Dev is the system that allows volunteers in our network to report their word of mouth activities to us to be reviewed and gain individualized feedback and response.

Here's how it works: We hire real human beings and educate them in the ways of word of mouth. They actually use their eyes and brains to read reports submitted by the volunteers who take part in our programs. The Com Devs evaluate each report, give it a numerical score based on several criteria, and then—and here's the amazing part—again, in a non-mechanized fashion, prepare a written response to the report to be delivered back to the volunteer. It's a highly labor-intensive process in an incredibly automated world.

Money people find this disturbing. "Here's what you do, Balter," they would say. "Just develop 50 standard replies, like, 'Jolly good show,' or 'This reminds me of *Don Quixote*.' You could have one Com Dev person do the work of the whole department. You could probably even write a program that would scan the report for keywords, pick the appropriate response, and automate the whole thing!" Several potential investors were so concerned about the Com Dev aspect—in particular, how we would scale it up if we grew fast—that they said, "Nuh-uh. No way."

What did we make of this?

No point in mincing words: Com Dev is the glue that holds the system together. It's what enables our network to grow organically and is the foundation that allows our entire process to succeed. It's what keeps BzzAgent from being just another destination for the deal-addict or freebie-hunter. And it gives us a system of effective measurement, without which no word of mouth network is complete. Here's why:

- COM DEV EMBODIES WHAT IT IS THAT ATTRACTS PEOPLE TO JOIN IN THE FIRST PLACE. People want to be listened to. They want their opinion to count. Yes, there are other perks, such as getting to try new products or gain insight and information before others do, but the real value is knowing that what you have to say is important. That your opinion is appreciated and valued. That you're not number 66bob*!A and perfect for sunscreen spamming.

In today's market, consumers are expecting companies to pay attention to what they have to say, and they want to support brands that consider their opinions the most valuable tool out there. When you answer the phone and hear the click/whir of an automated dialer you don't even wait for the telemarketer to say hello, you just hang up. It's why a site like www.Gethuman.com, which publishes the dialing codes of various customer service sites that enable you to bypass the infuriating phone tree and immediately get through to a real live person, gets more visitors than most customer service sites. Automated responses don't cut it anymore. We want to connect with real people who have the ability to interact with us and respond.

- **COM DEV ACCOMMODATES THE CHANGING NEEDS OF TODAY'S MARKETERS.** Marketing campaigns are much more unpredictable and have to be far more fluid than they were even 15 years ago. In those days, you'd develop your product, think up a tag line and establish a brand image, create your ad, buy your TV time, and off you went to market. Today, marketers manage in reverse. They develop their product, bring it to market, and then adapt their marketing and messaging to the consumers' reactions.

Com Dev provides marketers with the flexibility they require to make significant and substantive changes in mid-stream. Through Com Dev, companies can communicate with individuals when there's a big product boost—like when a major PR effort hits—or when there's a nasty product bump, like a recall. Com Dev enables companies to thank people, immediately, when they do something wonderful on their behalf—and then educate everyone else about that fabulous behavior.

- **COM DEV MAXIMIZES ROI.** One-on-one individualized responses allow us to help people become more effective product advocates. While many of us get the idea of how valuable our opinion is, being conscious of how to best share it is another concept altogether. Get this. An agent who interacts with Com Dev generates two to three times more word of mouth than the agent who doesn't.

Some things are meant to be automated. It's a whole lot easier getting money from an ATM than it is by waiting in line at the bank. Ron Popeil, inventor and pitchman, barked that you could "slice a tomato so thin it only has one side!" and sold 2 million Veg-O-matics.

Engaging in dialogue with customers isn't a good candidate for automation. It's not about how fast you can slice, dice, or mince those conversations.

Better to keep that tomato whole.

6. Everyone Deserves to Be Rewarded

YOU PROBABLY GO FOOD SHOPPING about once a week, which is just one of the reasons you don't starve. Due to familiarity and the fact that we're mainly creatures of habit, there's a pattern to the way you walk the aisles of your local supermarket—where you linger, which food counter you know to skip—and you may have even subconsciously noted which endcaps or open spaces are likely to have those tiny morsels of free cake or a station where you can gobble down an orange slice or two.

None of this is random.

Supermarkets have spent decades perfecting the art of aisle flow, and marketers will pay a premium to place their product in the high-traffic parts of the store where they can offer shoppers a little taste of their product for free. It's well worth the expense: Studies show that in-store sampling can cause seven out of 10 people to switch brands. (The other three would switch if they were actually involved with the brand, of course.)

On this particular day, let's say you come across a tray of smoked gouda cubes. You toothpick a couple into your mouth and go on your merry way. At home, while unpacking your food haul, your spouse (significant other/friend/sex buddy/whatever) asks if you found anything good. "Actually, yes," you say. "Amazing smoked gouda. Fabulous flavor. Gorgeous texture. We should get some for the party we're throwing on Saturday."

Now, choose the most likely response to this assertion:

1. **NONE.** Your spouse has no interest in cheese.
2. **RICH DISCUSSION.** Your buddy is fascinated by cheese, as are you, and you spend 20 minutes talking about mold forms and butterfat content.
3. **OUTRAGE.** Your significant other is horrified that you have sampled a cube of smoked cheese, sampled *anything* for that matter. He or she denounces you as an unprincipled "tryer" of free stuff and a martyr to the demonic intentions of unscrupulous marketers.

#1 and #2 are quite normal responses, and either is likely to occur. However, if you chose #3, I'd like to meet you, because you are the only person who has ever been excoriated for throwing a cube of smoked gouda down your gullet. Even if your partner worked for the anti-advertising magazine *Adbusters,* he or she would not likely be morally outraged that you had gobbled, and then recommended, that cheese.

However, there are those who bristle at the idea of rewarding people with products so they can talk about their merits with others in their social circles. Aren't they, in effect, being bribed? Won't they feel obligated to say only good things? Haven't they essentially sold their souls to the devil for a morsel of cheese?

Calm down.

Rewards have become a part of life. You receive Starwood Points for staying at a Sheraton, Westin, or W hotel, redeemable for upgrades to club floors or free additional stays. When you use your American Express card for a purchase, you are rewarded with access to airport lounges. Accumulate enough points and you can even cash them in for a ride on a subsonic flight or a cruise down the Nile. New kid on the way? Get a Upromise account and start spending to save for education. People can pile up rewards for buying groceries or cars on Memorial Day, flying in coach, procuring office supplies, filling a prescription, and pumping gas. We are rewarded so frequently that companies failing to reward customers are often at a serious disadvantage.

In 2007, Taco Bell offered a promotion where for one day, for a few hours, you could "steal a free taco" from them if a player stole a base during the Red Sox/Rockies World Series. Turns out a gutsy rookie named Jacoby Ellsbury did just that. Extra hot sauce for everyone. Jordan's, the furniture chain, made a gamble at the beginning of the major league baseball season. If you bought furniture from them on certain designated days, your entire payment would be waived if the Sox won the Series. (Which they did. Go Sox!)

So rewards are everywhere. But let's be clear: All rewards are not created equal.

In an experiment described in a scientific paper, *Effort of Payment*, researchers explored how people's behavior is affected by various forms of payment. A research subject asked a series of friends to help him load a sofa into a van and promised each one a different kind of reward. The researchers found that people were much more likely to help if they were offered a simple, non-cash reward like a bag of jellybeans or a pizza. The offer of cash immediately caused people to evaluate the task differently—not as a favor for a friend but as a work for hire. (Likely, they'll want more moolah 'cause your couch is so heavy, dammit.) A pizza is seen as a thank you among equals. A cash payment completely changes your relationship.

What does this have to do with word of mouth? The research shows that people often expend more effort if they're getting no payment at all than they would for a low cash payment. This is why I hate shill marketing so much. People are paid to act like they're enjoying a product, even if they're not. Suppose the sample guy at the supermarket offered you $5 to tell your friends you dug the gouda cube? You'd likely say, "No thanks."

So, rewards don't pollute the process. Cash does. That's why paying bloggers, whether in dollars or Krugerrands, is never going to generate the same authenticity of just letting them try a product on their own.

Cash is the ghost in the machine. It's what causes people to say and do things they normally wouldn't. Now if that doesn't give the hypocritical Starwood-carrying, AmEx-spending, free-rental-car-upgrade–loving, extra-iTunes-downloading, bonus-shot-of-coffee pundits something to talk about, then I don't know what will.

7. Word of Mouth Is (Not) for Losers

HIGH SCHOOL CAN BE A PRETTY BRUTAL PLACE. By the end of freshman year, you've been pegged—thanks to the way you dress, talk, where you live, and the music you listen to—as a member of some clique or subculture. Jock. Metalhead. Trekkie. Skate punk. Yuppie. Urbanite. Vegetarian. Vegan. Hippie. Gamer. Hacker. Hardliner.

And then there is the most damning category of all: Loser.

The life of the high school loser is one of rejection, exclusion, verbal ridicule, and physical assault. Last to be chosen for the softball team. First to be thrown into a snowbank at the bus stop. Loser status can cause scars that are still evident in adulthood. Poor self-image. Low self-esteem. Lack of confidence. Difficulty with forming relationships. Funny how so many losers, then, end up as winners. At a high school reunion you discover some who married supermodels, others who started huge investment banks, and one who even cured a hard-to-pronounce disease.

Marketers spend their lives identifying and pursuing their most-wanted customer segments, and loser is most assuredly not one of them. Losers have no social circles. If they talk at all, they talk to other losers. They will not help you build a brand. Better to get Diddy to hawk your product. Or a writer for the Engadget blog to give you some love. Almost anybody would be better than that loser from accounting, who brings in a bagged lunch of peanut butter and jelly on whole wheat (sans crusts) every day, and never, ever leaves his desk.

"Who the hell would sign up for a word of mouth network?" many a marketer has asked me (often the ones who haven't joined already). Anybody who has a life, so the cynic's rationale goes, would have better things to do with his or her time. After all, don't we all lead such incredibly hectic and action-packed lives that we barely have time to socialize with friends or chow down with the kids? People who take the time to participate in an organized word of mouth program must be looking to fill a huge hole in their lives.

Take this "argument" one step further. Since losers associate only with other losers, could it be that word of mouth networks are actually *loser magnets*? These must be the same people who take part in a focus group because they love the camaraderie and team spirit. They're the ones who hope that they get impaneled for jury duty to get to know others in their community.

The marketer's conclusion: *If I ever need to market a product to the loser community, I know just where to go.*

Here's a little experiment I'd like you to try. The next time you're gathered with some friends, ask them whether they'd join a word of mouth network. Would they get involved in trying new products and services and telling their friends about them?

There's a standard ratio. In a group of ten people, six of them will likely be *indifferents*. Talking about products is not part of their DNA, not something they would likely do on a regular basis. But they see no harm in it.

There will usually be one *naysayer*. The idea irritates him, grosses him out. He sees this as a disaster scenario. The end of trust. A sign of desperation on the part of the participant *and* the marketer. Everyone involved should be ashamed. Surely this is one step away from some kind of final solution of complete commercialization. The next thing we know, marketers will have burrowed into the very folds of our brains and be controlling our every thought and purchase.

I have found there is no point in trying to convert the indifferents or convince the naysayers.

The key is to find the three of the ten who are the *supporters*. Try new stuff? Have brands listen to their comments? Influence the product marketing process? The idea excites and attracts them.

Now I can reveal that, at first, we were a little worried that we had created a loser network inhabited by the leftovers of a deteriorating society. But when we began to look more closely at our supporters, we saw they were not losers:

- **STEVE COOK**, a VP of Worldwide Innovation at Coca Cola (now at Samsung), signed up early on. He wanted to get involved with brands at a deeper level.

- **LENORE FISCHER,** an IT consultant and part-time blogger.
- **JEFF GLASS,** previously CEO of M-Qube, a mobile marketing company which was sold for a cool $250 million, and now a partner at Bain Capital.
- **JASON DESJARDINS,** manager of the dairy section of a supermarket in New Hampshire, and one of the most articulate guys you'll ever meet.
- **MITCH CAPLAN,** one of the first champions of big marketers's spending on empowering the consumer, and now the Chief Marketing Officer of Young & Rubicam, the communications conglomerate.

We were pleased to find that our network has its share of winners, but we then began to realize that what we had been looking for may not have mattered at all.

Research shows that "key influencers"—those people with extremely large and active social networks—may not be all they're cracked up to be for marketers. One researcher at Miami University found that marketers who devote an inordinate amount of resource to connecting with influencers may actually limit the success of their marketing efforts. He writes, "Marketers need to realize that the majority of their audience, not just the well-connected few, is eager and willing to pass along well-designed and relevant messages."

Other research suggests that the effectiveness of word of mouth does not depend on who's doing the talking. Duncan Watts, a professor at Columbia University, argues that marketers should "focus less on who people influence and more on how people are influenced." Watts' research confirms my belief that marketers should spend less time on signing up influentials and more time finding people who might be passionate about their brands—and then helping them become aware and knowledgeable about how to communicate with others who might share their passion.

Despite the research and the arguments to the contrary, many marketers still make the assumption that people in word of mouth networks must be a bunch of people with whom they'd rather not associate.

So let me define who it is that joins a word of mouth network, and why. It has nothing to do with losers or influentials, how busy your life is, or whether you're on a quest for belonging. Supporters tend to be people who have opinions and are aware they have them, who think it's fun to be involved with brands and products, and who like brands to understand that supporters have power because they can choose which brands to advocate. They don't care much about the "free stuff" (in fact, in our surveys, agents rank "free stuff" second-to-last of 14 reasons for joining a word of mouth network). They like to be informed. They're curious. They are among millions of people who do not think it's sinful to be interested in and like products.

Like all of us, agents are sometimes winners and sometimes losers. You were voted Most Likely to Succeed in high school, but you just got fired from your day job. You lost a ton of money in the stock market, but now you're making big bucks. You spilled coffee on your nice white turtleneck before you picked up your blind date. But then again in high school you were voted most likely to become president. The dog peed on the new rug. Your kid got into the college of his choice.

We're all winners and we're all losers. Those particular classifications have little to do with how we experience products or why we talk about them.

III. WHAT YOU MUST KNOW
(in practice)

If you have five months with nothing else to do, why not hike the Appalachian trail? "Thru hikers" always begin the journey in early spring so they have a chance to complete the 2,200 miles from southern Georgia to northern Maine before the snow flies.

There are the purists who doggedly walk every inch and climb every summit of the main trail. There are the Blue Blazers, who occasionally take the short-cuts that are marked with blue blazes. And then there are the Yellow Blazers, who are not above hitchhiking when the spirit moves and opportunity arises.

If you're serious about taking the walk, you'll need to prepare. Run 10 miles a day. Tone up the abs, quads, and glutes. Do that crawl thing the army guys do under barbed wire. Take eight-hour practice hikes with a 35-pound pack. Break in a kick-ass pair of hiking boots. Stock up on well-cushioned moisture-wicking socks.

No matter how well you prepare, you'll be sure to encounter hazards that can derail you along the way. Ticks carrying Lyme disease. Poison ivy. Violent storms. Ravenous bears. Thirst. Boredom. Loneliness. Cramps. Even those who survive all these challenges can be defeated by the "killer mile," an in-credibly tough stretch of boulder-strewn trail not far from the finish line.

I'm glad to report, however, that of the 30,000 people who have been tough enough to complete the entire journey, only one contracted hantavirus, a rare rodent-borne disease that pretty much wrecks the lungs.

1. There Are No Shortcuts

GARY BROLSMA'S NUMA NUMA dance may go down in web history as one of the most memorable viral videos ever.

Yet, even with some 700 million views, it's far from the most watched viral video of all time. That distinction falls to the baffling display of homegrown Japanese-style Naginata stick fighting by the so-called Star Wars Kid, who achieved, according to the measurement firm Viral Factory, about 900 million views.

Nevertheless, Gary beat out the Kid as the poster child for viral success. His video, whose soundtrack is the song "Dragostea Din Tea" by the Romanian pop band O-Zone, and whose visuals are inspired by Japanese flash animation, was released in December 2004, and within two years it had been viewed by people around the world many millions of times. Gary characterized himself to *The New York Times* as an "unwilling and embarrassed celebrity," but still agreed to make appearances on the *Tonight Show* and *Good Morning America* and gained mild fame on VH1's *Best Week Ever*. There were endless parodies of the Numa Numa dance, as well, by Lego, GI Joe, Resident Evil, and Napoleon Dynamite, and some nut job even created a dance featuring John F. Kennedy Jr.

Seven hundred million, 900 million—when you reach that kind of saturation, the difference is insignificant. Most companies would be more than content to get a few million views for their viral efforts. To get into the 10th most watched viral spot, *The Shining Redux* captured more than 50 million views. It would cost many hundreds of thousands of dollars of traditional media to get the same exposure that Diet Coke and Mentos received from the 6 million views of the consumer-generated Eepy Bird experiment that featured both of their products.

Gary may have considered himself an unwilling celebrity, but that doesn't mean he didn't enjoy being in the spotlight. Two years after he had amazed the world with his shaking and air-stabbing, he resurfaced with a professionally produced video called New Numa. Its release was accompanied by a contest in which $25,000 would be given to one lucky viewer. While some people were intrigued by Gary's second act, and more than a few showed up to try to nab the cash, New Numa had nowhere near the impact of the original. By early 2007, Gary and his Numas were little more than a bit of cyber nostalgia.

Don't read too much into this, but did you notice what Gary is wearing in the video? Squeezed onto his head is a pair of cheap black headphones, suggesting that he wanted to keep his dance moves private and didn't want to wake up the parents. There's only one article of clothing that can be clearly seen—a nondescript T-shirt, likely size XXL. I have studied this shirt closely and I see no branding on it. No Nike swoosh. No P. Diddy/Sean

Combs/Puffy logo. Nothing. Most marketers would have given an arm and a leg for a cross sell or T-shirt–based sponsorship.

Gary captured lightning in a bottle and there wasn't a brand in sight.

The Tiny Little Alligator That Roared

A number of memorable tennis players have captured the world's attention over the last century.

Björn Borg had fabulous hair, a killer headband—and an unbeatable name. Arthur Ashe was classy and graceful. John McEnroe had a lot of heart (and was a bit of a drama queen). But only one had enough style and passion to earn the nickname "Le Crocodile" or "The Alligator" for his antics on the court. With an aggressive, confrontational, and belligerent attitude, that honor could only be bestowed on Jean Rene Lacoste.

If you don't follow tennis, you probably won't recognize the name, but you may make the connection to Rene's most enduring claim to fame: the Lacoste tennis shirt. He invented it in 1929 and immediately began wearing it during match play. Some four years later, the collared shirt in the piqué cotton knit had gained enough attention and praise that Lacoste founded *La Société Chemise Lacoste* to sell the shirts to the public. They were easily identified by their logo, a tiny alligator on the left breast, with his mouth slightly open and something of a smirk in his eye. (Not sure how they pulled that off, but look closely and you'll see what I mean.) The genius of Lacoste's innovation should not be overlooked; this was the first time in history that a brand logo had appeared on the outside of an article of clothing. The fashion industry was forever changed.

By 1951, the company was producing the shirts in a wide range of colors and had added a variety of other items to the line as well, such as shirts for sailors and golfers. In 1952, Lacoste clothing was exported to the United States for the first time and promoted as "the status symbol for the competent sportsman." In the 1970s, Rene's son Bernard became the steward of the Lacoste brand, and he helped to make the tennis shirt a must-have item for the preppy set. As the brand reached new heights of popularity, the company created new products and brand extensions, including watches, leather goods, and walking shoes.

As with all good brands, an underground rumor even began to circulate—that the company made a tennis shirt in size 2, which translates into an XXS. Tininess was worth talking about.

The shirt was so successful that knockoffs were inevitable. In the 1980s, the Lacoste brand found itself competing against upstarts like Polo and Le Tigre clothing. Boast, another clothing company, created a version for the underground, stoner set, featuring a pot leaf where the crocodile was supposed to be.

But by the 1990s, Lacoste had been pretty much relegated to

the nostalgia pile. If people owned an alligator shirt and actually put it on, they usually wore it underneath something else, like a sweater and quilted parka. Ralph Lauren's tiny polo player and pony were *en vogue*. After 60 years, the alligator was out. It found itself dancing with the same threat of total irrelevance that the Numa Numa kid would encounter nearly a decade later. But while both experienced a dramatic fall from grace, there was one important distinction. Lacoste, unlike Gary, didn't go away. It merely hibernated, awaiting the great resurgence it would accomplish nearly a decade later.

By 2005, Lacoste had been re-engineered, modernized, and re-energized. Fifty million of its products were sold that year alone, in over 110 countries. Several young tennis stars, including Andy Roddick, were now wearing its products on the court. You couldn't miss the logo in snapshots of Scottish golfer Colin Montgomerie chipping out of a sand trap; other famous athletes soon became Lacoste enthusiasts. The trend hunters paid attention. Rappers like Kanye West were pushing past the velvet ropes of the nightclub scene proudly wearing the alligator.

By 2006, Lacoste was on such a rapid climb that it was able to license extensions to best-of-breed partners like luggage maker Samsonite, who added Lacoste to its $1 billion portfolio alongside Timberland and Alexander McQueen. Suddenly, alligators were everywhere.

While the differences between the Numa Numa kid and Lacoste are vast, this is more than just a tale of the chunky kid and the athletic alligator. Lacoste, a brand that had been left for dead, took a second shot at success and hit the mark. Gary Brolsma, on the other hand, fizzled miserably when he tried to re-energize his "brand," even though it was recognized by millions and had incredible distribution across the web.

The difference?

Numa Numa captured the fleeting essence of virality, while Lacoste harnessed the true power of word of mouth.

What Is It You're Searching For?

Ever since Hotmail appeared on the scene and showed that one consumer can influence many, many others, brands have been chasing the kind of viral explosion that catapulted the Numa Numa dance to web glory.

Steve Jurvetson, a partner at venture capital firm Draper Fisher Jurvetson (DFJ), has often been credited for coining the term "viral marketing." But Jeffrey Rayport, a professor at the Harvard Business School, was the first to document the early thinking about the concept. In a 1996 article for *Fast Company* magazine called "The Virus of Marketing," Rayport described the concept of how ideas spread around a network of consumers.

Hotmail, a company that DFJ funded, applied that thinking by adding a message about its service to the bottom of each of its members' outbound emails, thus prompting others to click to get their own account—and the "virus" of marketing began to spread. Consumer conversations could create incredible results, and people flocked to the Hotmail service by the millions. The company was able to kick back and watch it happen. It's no wonder that *every* marketer on the planet soon wanted to create some viral mojo of their own.

Many follow-on viral attempts hit some pretty serious road bumps along the way. They discovered that almost *any* viral communication can explode with extraordinary power and speed, but that not *every* communication will do so. They're just not that easy to create. For every concept that has successfully gone viral, tens of thousands have floundered and disappeared into obscurity. Viral marketing turned out to be a hit-or-miss business, just like piloting a TV show or picking the numbers to win the lottery.

It's nearly impossible to deliberately *create* something that is guaranteed to go viral. You need the right product, the right type of consumers paying attention, and perfect timing. Many marketers may tell you they know the formula for success. They don't. The best they can do is "luck you" into a little virality.

Even those who do get lucky usually run up against another problem. Let's say you actually find the magic; you find a way to inspire millions of consumers to immediately pay attention to your brand and consume it through a viral activity. Thanks to the very nature of that activity—its explosiveness and immediacy—you have probably created an overnight success. While that sounds pretty glorious, don't be fooled: This is exactly where the trouble begins. If you've created that much growth that quickly, you now find yourself staring into the Numa Numa abyss. You may become a fad whose rapid rise to stardom will be complemented by an equally speedy fall from grace.

It's incredibly rare that a company can make the transition from viral escalation to long-term acceptance of its product or brand. Hotmail is one of the lucky few; today, there are still millions of people who use Hotmail. This is partly because Microsoft purchased Hotmail and poured a lot of money and energy into improving the service.

But the real secret of Hotmail's sustained success is not the viral explosion it experienced at the beginning, but rather the steady stream of word of mouth that flowed around it. The folks in Redmond immediately localized the service for people around the globe and capitalized on the base they had built. They constantly made Hotmail easier and easier to use and made sure that there was always something worth talking about.

(Microsoft did eventually lose steam with Hotmail. The company forgot to re-register the domain name in 1999, which left millions of people without the service for nearly two months. That put

Hotmail on the Top 40 list, for sure—for all the wrong reasons.)

As the story of Hotmail demonstrates, true word of mouth is about engaging individuals for the long term, so that they continue to support and engage in dialogue about a brand at the moments when others are most receptive. It's neither as glorious nor as memorable as a well-executed viral event, but it's what determines long-term success.

Viral marketing is empowered by the incredible force of thousands upon thousands of people talking all at once. It's the incredible acceleration, the speed at which it moves, that is an indication of its success. Word of mouth, on the other hand, relies on the power of thousands of thousands of people—maybe the very same ones—having conversations with multiple people over a long period of time. It's about endurance and long-term sustainability, about a product that continues to deliver, and remains front of mind, leaving people to share messages about it on many occasions in many different ways. Put simply, viral marketing is a 50-yard wind sprint; word of mouth is a 26-mile marathon.

Many people confuse word of mouth with viral activity but the two are very different. The viral success is one that seems to stop the world. There's a huge, startling Aha! moment—a thunderclap accompanied by a bolt of lightning scorching out of the sky.

When word of mouth is really working for you, the quiet and calm can be a little alarming. The slow build of the Lacoste brand, for example, led to massive sales in the 1970s and an appearance in *The Yuppie Handbook* in the 1980s, the culmination of a trend that peaked nearly 40 years after it started. Its resurgence as a retro brand took another 20 years. "You gotta check out Lacoste's viral video," wasn't the harbinger of its comeback. There was no massive marketing explosion. Just a simple, slow-moving, and consistent approach to making clothes that were worth wearing.

The former CMO of a major sneaker company once said to me, "Agencies and marketers are a bunch of sheep, with a few exceptions." His explanation for this rather harsh assessment was that the results of marketing efforts are usually evaluated within the same quarter they're implemented, so anything that requires more than three months to implement and complete is a hard sell for the CMO. They need the quick hit, the smell and perception that whatever they're doing is taking off; they need approval in the boardroom and the eyes of shareholders. Which is what makes viral marketing so attractive: It can keep a CMO afloat for another quarter.

If it works, that is.

Word of mouth may build more slowly than viral, but it too can get results within a single quarter. According to McKinsey & Company, 76 percent of all purchase decisions are impacted by word of mouth. Keller Fay estimates there are some 3.4 billion word of mouth conversations each day and 2.3 billion of those are about brands.

Word of mouth has breadth and scale and, when it takes off, can create long-lasting brand loyalty among consumers. Word of mouth generates advocates and even fanatics, but don't expect it to turn consumers into a hungry, howling mob overnight. Your servers won't melt in a this-one-goes-to-eleven type of way.

So there's a fork in the road ahead. Which path will you take?

1. Go for the quick hit and play the odds that you might be one of the very, very lucky few.
2. Focus your energy on building the foundation that will lead to long term evangelism.

Are you a gambler or a pragmatist?

Laying the Word of Mouth Foundation

If you've decided that the shortest-path, betting-man's route of viral marketing is your choice, you might think you can skip this next section.

But don't jump ahead just yet. Even if you do strike viral gold, you'll still need to figure out how to maintain the energy and passion of what you've created. You'll need the tools to make sure your viral flare-up doesn't dissipate.

The other (better) route, of course, is to focus on developing a strong word of mouth foundation from the start.

As a discipline, word of mouth is probably unlike anything

you've done before, and you're going to have to think differently about how you market with it. Don't think of word of mouth as an event. It's a process and it needs to be embedded in everything you do, so that it can enable the telling of your story in multiple ways. Nor is it a linear narrative of the kind you tell in a product launch or a blockbuster Superbowl commercial. Think of it as a three-dimensional dialogue.

Apple's iPod launch, for example, was enabled by the decades of stories of the company's successful and not-so-successful innovation, stupendous advertising, and the participation of a charismatic leader. The Rio PMP300 and the Compaq Personal Jukebox, MP3 players with very similar features to the iPod, were released nearly five years before Apple's player, yet struggled to gain much attention.

The stronger and broader your foundation is, the more capacity you'll have to create a multitude of dialogues of the kind that lead to word of mouth success.

For mainstream musicians, the ultimate validation of their work and careers can be found in Cleveland, Ohio. That's where they can join the likes of Led Zeppelin, Madonna, and James Brown as members of the Rock and Roll Hall of Fame. Artists are eligible for induction 25 years after the release of their first record, and must have subsequently demonstrated that they played a significant role in the history of rock and roll.

Falco becomes eligible in 2008, but it's unlikely he'll make the cut. You may remember Falco as the genius behind the song "Rock Me Amadeus," released in 1985. The song became an instant hit in the United States (Falco was already popular in Germany and Austria) and just about every warm-blooded teen in the country watched his video. But, although Falco tried mightily to come up with another hit, he could never repeat the phenomenon of "Amadeus." If you didn't buy the record but want to take a listen, check out VH1's *100 All Time Greatest One Hit Wonders* (Falco's #44).

Contrast Falco to the Grateful Dead, a group who began playing live music in the mid-1960s. They built a reputation for long shows, wild jamming, and impressive musicianship that helped them grow into one of the biggest touring acts of all time. Unlike Falco, The Dead didn't particularly care about creating A Big Hit. They had no particular interest in trying to generate the one song that would reach #1 on Casey Kasem's *American Top 40*. As a matter of fact, they didn't have a certifiable hit until 1987, 20 years after they started playing—"Touch of Grey," which reached #1 on Billboard's Mainstream Rock list. Yet the Grateful Dead has gone down in history as one of the greatest rock bands of all time and was inducted into the Rock and Roll Hall of Fame in 1994.

How did that happen? It was more than just listening to the music play: The Dead planned, developed, and sustained a remarkable word of mouth foundation. Their lore consisted and still consists of a multitude of stories and parables that could be characterized by a saying that is common among their most loyal fans, "There is nothing like a Grateful Dead concert."

There are the stories, for example, of The Dead as technology pioneers. In the 1970s, unhappy with the sound systems of most venues, the band combined the best stereophonic sound systems—89 300-watt solid-state and three 350-watt vacuum-tube amplifiers generating a total of 26,400 watts RMS of audio power—to create the highest-quality concert experience available at the time. They called it simply the Wall of Sound. It boomed The Dead's songs to audience members at the back of any 70,000 seat arena and the music even sounded pretty damn good a quarter mile away. The Wall of Sound was so physically enormous and so complicated to set up, the band had to have two of them, which they deployed like tiddlywinks. While they played their gig one night, the road crew was setting up the Wall of Sound at the next venue for the following night's show.

The Dead knew how to build their stories through conversations with their fans. They allowed people to record their shows when others wouldn't, which created a community of Deadheads who freely shared the band's music. The band traveled to Egypt in 1978 to play at the Pyramids; Bill Walton of the Boston Celtics had a broken leg at the time, so he hopped the bus and went on tour with them. They were inclusive in their music, jamming with every musician you can imagine from Gregg Allman to Etta James, from Steve Miller to Branford Marsalis.

The stories were personal, too. Jerry Garcia's constant battles with heroin addiction and fast-food binges, as unfortunate as they were, generated vast amounts of speculative dialogue. After ballooning to some 300 pounds in the mid-1980s, Garcia's bad habits put him into a diabetic coma in 1986. He finally got the message and went on a health kick. At the end of the decade, concertgoers witnessed him actually bending at the waist and reaching down to adjust the foot pedals for his guitar. Even that was worth talking about.

The Dead created energy and word of mouth through the glut of experiences and stories that allowed their ideas to spread far and wide. Sound fanatics loved to talk about their technical experiments. Musicians knew when the band was jamming with somebody and passed along the news. Historians wondered who this hippie outfit might be that had set up shop outside the Great Pyramid.

Regardless of whether you groove to The Dead's music, it's clear they created an audience and attitude that had made them one of the most successful, longest-lasting, and highest-grossing rock bands in history. They didn't look for the shortcut; they didn't try to create the hit. They created a foundation that would last for the long term.

I won't even ask whether you'd rather be Falco or the Grateful Dead, or at least the equivalent of either of them. The relevant question is not which one you'd rather be, but how you apply the word of mouth foundation techniques to your own organization. Developing long-term evangelism and creating sustainable dialogues are worthy goals for every marketer and company.

Companies are predicted to spend more on "conversational media" (as word of mouth is sometimes called) than on traditional media by 2012. Even if it takes a decade longer than that, now is the time to start planning for the changing landscape.

Foundations aren't built overnight.

Optimizing the Core

Sometime around the beginning of time, Eve offered Adam an apple, and so word of mouth began.

"It's the oldest medium on the planet," a word of mouth service provider will gush, with a gleam in the eye. Over the years, word of mouth has morphed and norms have changed, but the basic idea has remained the same. Word of mouth practitioners talk about, and often recommend, that shiny apple to someone else. The hard part today, of course, is knowing just how to make the offer effectively.

The modern word of mouth era began early in the 21st century, when companies began looking for ways to help consumers "pass the apple," or at least word of the apple, to others. There was little for-malized knowledge about the medium, much of what was published was wrong or misguided, and there was no roadmap for deploying word of mouth as a scalable and measurable medium.

Companies were on their own to experiment and tinker. Lots of them found that word of mouth has many, many paths it can follow. It's not as simple as just "grabbing some" when the time is right, but rather about developing and maintaining a deep under-standing of how word of mouth really works—about how to build a word of mouth foundation, managing word of mouth as a pro-cess, and recognizing that word of mouth is a medium that needs to be deployed, adapted, and constantly optimized.

It's also necessary to understand that word of mouth is opti-mized by the cast of characters that surround the brand and help to make the stories meaningful and relevant. Rene Lacoste stayed close to the Lacoste business for many years, acting as de facto spokesman, inspiring the workforce, and establishing rela-tionships with celebrities and advocates who would embrace the brand with as much fervor and conviction as Rene did. The Dead were special because of the family group they created. It included fans all over the world, as well as colorful personalities like Dan Healy, the technician who helped revolutionize their sound, and Baba Olatunji, the Nigerian drummer who helped them explore new rhythms live, onstage, with tens of thousands listening in.

To build a strong word of mouth foundation you need people who are inspired to be a part of the experiences that build your identity, and to share experiences with those around them. It wasn't just about Jerry or Rene, but about everyone else who believed so much in what those central figures were doing.

Throwing Open the Doors

In late 2003, in the early days of corporate blogging, BzzAgent launched the BeeLog (blog.bzzagent.com).

Corporate blogs marked the beginning of a major change in the way companies communicated with their consumers. Blogs gave them the ability to describe their expertise and constantly refine and adapt their messages in real time as the environment shifted. Blogs were also more flexible and immediate and gave companies the ability to respond to people and issues quickly and frequently—every day, every minute, every hour—in a way they could not with press articles, white papers, or other traditional communications media.

We understood these wonderful qualities of the blog, but we didn't intend to use ours as a way to talk about theories of consumer dialogue or our nascent industry. Rather, we saw the BeeLog as a perfect testing ground for the behaviors and patterns of word of mouth. We had already gone a long way to developing our word of mouth foundation, but we still needed to optimize our word of mouth core.

As part of our optimization, we knew we needed to develop a perspective worth talking about and we decided it would be transparency—true, unencumbered organizational openness. We strongly believed, and still do believe, that transparency is good for companies and their relationships with their communities.

We decided that we would throw open the doors in a way that few companies would ever dare. It would enable us to push the boundaries and norms of corporate secrecy and we'd learn how transparency would change the behavior of the market, our clients, and our employees. And we believed that, ultimately, we would gain a better understanding of the workings of word of mouth itself.

We quickly found the pursuit of transparency to be nerve-wracking. We started simply, by posting some presentations and a few of our early emails on the BeeLog. The postings were public and available to anybody who knew about the blog or happened upon it. But we were cautious about what kinds of things to post and how much to share, and that meant we weren't making much progress on optimizing our core.

After almost a year of this kind of hesitant dance, we finally took the leap. We publicly documented a struggle that the leadership team was having about which of two candidates to choose for an important senior sales position in the company.

One of the candidates, we were confident, could handle the

challenges of the job in his sleep, and happened to be so good-looking that all the women in the office giggled when he walked down the hall. We nicknamed him The Ringer.

The other candidate also seemed to be a good fit—but made it clear that he hoped to become president of the company someday. We didn't have a president at the time and weren't seeking one, but we did like the idea of adding presidential-caliber bench strength. We dubbed this guy El Presidente.

The senior management team had endless debates about whether we needed a president now or ever would need one, which sidetracked the discussion about which candidate would be best for the sales position. At last, we turned to our transparency tool and put up a post about our quandary on the BeeLog. We invited the world into the dialogue. We posted the bios of each candidate (with their names removed), explained our dilemma, and asked readers to help us decide which person to hire.

Yikes!

The post opened up all kinds of issues beyond the hiring furor. Because we had grown quickly, and we had added layers of management, many staff members felt that they no longer had access to important information about the company. The blog posting gave them an opening to tell us about what they saw happening in the company and which candidate they thought was best suited for the job.

We realized that one of the most important functions of our word of mouth initiative could be to help maintain our culture as the company grew. It could inspire employees to remain involved, to better understand the business, and to see it from perspectives different from their own.

In *The Wisdom of Crowds*, James Surowiecki argues that decisions that are based on the aggregation of information in groups are often better than the ones that might have been made by any single member of that group. He couldn't have been more right. The collected wisdom of the BeeLog posters was that we should hire The Ringer. Their view was that he was the right guy for the position we needed filled, and that we should not worry about some possible future need.

I ignored the wisdom of the crowd and went for El Presidente, seeking to build the bench strength for later growth. He was a nice enough guy, but a corporate disaster from the moment he walked in the door. He lasted 89 days before it was obvious to everyone that he had to go. We immediately got in touch with The Ringer, but of course some other company had snapped him up.

So what about our core? We learned that throwing open the doors doesn't do any good unless you listen to the voices coming in.

Letting Outsiders In

Our initial foray into transparency was fraught with concerns and issues, successes and disappointments. It certainly gave people a reason to talk about us. But most important, it allowed us to conceptualize which elements drive word of mouth and which don't.

We continued to tinker with transparency.

In early 2006, our business was on the brink of a major transition. We had raised a good chunk of venture capital, which brought us a new board of directors and enabled us to take on a slew of new tasks. It seemed a perfect time to continue our experiments in transparency and to further develop our core.

We invited an author, John Butman, to spend 90 days in our offices and blog about everything and anything he found interesting or worthy of note. He would have access to everybody who was willing to talk to him (anybody could decline to talk or be mentioned in the blog) and could poke into files, offices, and corporate information pretty much as he pleased. Unlike the BeeLog, this was not meant to be an exercise in self-evaluation. We wanted to hear an outsider's unbiased perspective on our business and our company. The experiment was called *90 Days of BzzAgent* (90days.bzzagent.com).

Butman visited us virtually every day, and would spend his hours wandering around the office, having conversations with staff, often becoming their sounding board. He scratched fervently on notepads during client meetings, questioned sales guys about their travels, and dipped into hundreds of reports from our agents.

He pulled no punches. He wrote of executive conflict, growing pains, our weight-loss challenge (I didn't win), and our debates over how to spend (or save) $13.8 million of investor capital.

After some initial caution and skepticism, people began to thrive on the content. On day 75, Butman wrote, "Everybody wants *90 Days* to reveal the real and ultimate truth about BzzAgent, as they see it." We realized that what kept many people intrigued and connected to the experiment was its perspective on them. It wasn't so much about the risk we were taking; rather, it was about how *90 Days* gave people a chance to be a part of the bigger picture. Inclusiveness has since become one of our word of mouth tenets.

One important learning of the *90 Days* experiment was around "talkability"—the likelihood that something would be considered worth talking about. In particular, we wanted to know which aspects of transparency would generate dialogue. When Butman wrote about executive conflict, it prompted very little response. We were exposing ourselves, but nobody much cared. The same was true of employee profiles and analysis of our image in the media.

But when he wrote a piece about pests—people who we realized were taking advantage of the BzzAgent community and its system—the floodgates opened. The subject of pests, it seemed, had a very high talkability quotient (and probably some inclusiveness, too).

We discovered that subjects that polarized people drove the

most dialogue. They often felt morally or intellectually obligated to express their point of view. For example, Butman wrote about rewards and how they might be complicating the natural equation of word of mouth. It proved to be a highly polarizing topic and caused a barrage of input from our agents, vendors, clients, and employees. The result of the post was profound, creating a deep introspection into our rewards process, and ultimately leading to changes in it. Even more important, we gained some invaluable experience in how to create and manage polarization to generate word of mouth.

The *90 Days* experiment also confirmed my belief that word of mouth spreads more quickly and with greater energy if there is a real, or perceived, sense of a time limit. We made it very clear that Butman would be blogging for 90 days and 90 days only. This created a palpable sense of urgency. What issues would he write about? Which would be ignored? Who would be mentioned? What stories would he tell? People also talked with avid interest about the timeframe itself. Why was it only 90 days? If it worked, would we keep it?

Everything we tried, and every test of the boundary that we established, helped us further understand the components that make word of mouth work. One reason we involve ourselves in such projects is to keep exploring what works and what doesn't.

Before you can truly implement word of mouth, you have to

develop a foundation and then optimize your core. Then once these fundamentals are in place it's time to master the next step in the word of mouth process: applying the tools you've developed and refined.

It's a little like going to a wedding, and voyeuristically studying people's moves on the dance floor. While some may have learned how to shake their hips and flap their arms, many clearly haven't figured out how to put it all together. Stick around for a rousing version of the Chicken Dance or Let's Go Crazy and you'll be able to quickly judge who hasn't figured that part out. It's not pretty.

Tapping the Word of Mouth Stream

The movie *Ghostbusters*, released in 1984, became an instant classic. You may not remember (or may want to forget) that moviegoers actually got up and danced in the aisles to the theme song, *Who's Afraid of Those Ghosts?* But you probably do remember the climax, which involved a showdown between a 100-foot-tall Stay Puft Marshmallow Man and the ghost-busting squad. When all their usual weapons failed, the Ghostbusters did the unthinkable. They fired their Proton Packs at the Marshmallow Man, thus causing a crossing of protoplasmic streams, which common Ghostbusting knowledge suggested could lead to global catastrophe. Surprisingly, it produced a "total protonic reversal" instead, which destroyed the ferocious and gloopy attacker and saved the day.

What do the Ghostbusters have to do with word of mouth, you ask? Not much, but bear with me a moment.

The Ghostbusting squad had spent virtually the entire film preparing for that great finale. In the course of neutralizing dozens of ghosts, they had fired their proton streams hundreds of times. They had tested all their equipment and learned what would and wouldn't be effective in catching those pesky ghosts. Only then, after all of the hard work and preparation, were they able to understand how to effectively cross their protonic streams to create a result of value, rather than cause destructive chaos. In essence, they built their foundation and established their core—and then were able to use the tools they had created to tap into the stream.

Word of mouth works the same way.

From the outside, word of mouth seems like an awfully easy channel to tap into. Just get a bunch of consumers together and give them a reason to talk to each other. But the reality is that the power of the medium is affected by the most subtle of social norms. It's about how we talk to each other and what makes us willing to share our opinions, which makes it a more flexible and fluid medium than any other.

Many of the skills and techniques of traditional media aren't applicable to word of mouth. Once you understand the medium, it doesn't mean you can or should drink from the hose at all times. It's necessary to learn how to work with your customers, how to inspire them or reward them or make them feel part of your organization. And those methods need to be continuously evolved and refined.

*

Imagine you are Joey Chestnut, entering the Coney Island Hot Dog eating contest. Your challenge: Beat the six-time defending world champion Takeru "Tsunami" Kobayashi.

How would you prepare? Would you decide a month before that you needed to learn how to gobble hot dogs and buns by the dozens, or would you start a year out, thinking about how to best prepare your body for the onslaught? You'd likely need to stretch your stomach out, and figure out a good swallowing technique. You'd need to put your body in a position to win. You'd need a foundation that could give you the greatest chance of success.

But even with that very fine foundation you're going to have to practice. Yes, you've stretched out the stomach muscles, but you still have to understand which techniques work and which don't. You might try eating sweets to determine if the high blood sugar levels will open your pylorus (the passage between your stomach and duodenum) so you can cram more down there. Or maybe you'll practice dipping your buns in water to make them easier to swallow. You might fast. Or meditate. Kobayashi eats cabbage. One contestant practiced by challenging actual dogs to eating races.

And once you've learned all the techniques and prepared your body for the onslaught, then and only then do you turn to the competition itself. It's at that moment that you're going to need to consider which methods to use, and in which order. You'll recognize which approaches were best in practice but aren't particularly useful in this particular challenge.

It will go down in history that Joey Chestnut unseated the champion Kobayashi by eating 66 hot dogs and buns in 12 minutes, no doubt due to the preparation of developing a foundation and the practice of understanding what would help him succeed.

If it was necessary for Joey Chestnut to put in that much preparation and practice to win a hot dog eating contest, how can you expect to master word of mouth and apply it as needed without doing the same?

RANDOM BONUSES ARE WORTH TALKING ABOUT

As a staff writer at the *Daily Nexus*, University of Southern California's school newspaper, Brendan Buhler snagged the last interview that Douglas Adams, author of *The Hitchhiker's Guide to the Galaxy*, ever gave.

Alumni of Columbia University's daily newspaper include Herman Wouk, Jack Kerouac, Tony Kushner, and Langston Hughes. At Wayne State University, a guest columnist wrote a piece titled "Islam Sucks" in February 2002, which set off a storm of controversy across the globe. That same year, the team at *Cornell Review* published a column by Elliott Reed about a cover-up at the campus health center where vibrators were being sold under the counter.

During my college career, I co-wrote a column for the *Skidmore Scope* titled "Mike & Dave's Room," which won no awards, broke no big stories, and was published on what would best be called an erratic schedule. Mainly, Mike and I had a great time getting together and cracking ourselves up about the brands, products, and services of our childhood years. Big Wheels, Toucan Sam, Sit 'n Spin, Barbapapa, Underdog.

We thought we were being irreverent, sleep-deprived, partied-out college students. Now I see that we were giving brands the highest compliment they could ever receive. We talked about them.

1. Mike & Dave's Room: Feb. 21, 1991

HELLO ONCE AGAIN, our brothers and sisters. Before we dig into our Necco Wafers, we'd like to apologize for last week's absence. During this time, the investigative staff at Mike & Dave's room has been diligently probing into a world seldom seen, the world of breakfast cereal legends who have fallen from grace. Be forewarned . . . it is not a pretty picture we are about to paint. We have seen some things that will shatter the wholesome images that these shifty characters (Zim) have portrayed to the youth of America for years. After gaining this information, we feel that some of the innocence of childhood has been lost. One of the many cereal legends that we found hid a dark sinister half is none other than Captain Wilber Samuel Crunch.

Captain Crunch has always appeared to the youth of America as a man of faith and justice. A man possessing a higher wisdom. A crusader for the crunchy cause. But on November 3, 1990, the Captain's world crumbled around him. At 11:37 P.M. the police received a call from one of the Crunch's neighbors reporting a disturbance from next door. When arriving on the scene at the Crunch's Santa Monica dream home, the officers reported hearing shouts and cries of protest. Upon breaking down the door, they were both shocked and disgusted at the sight before them.

Apparently, that night, Mr. Crunch went out drinking with two naval buddies, Captain Stubing of *Love Boat* fame, and his long-time comrade, Captain Morgan. After an evening of grotesque debauchery, the Captain returned home extremely intoxicated and violent. He proceeded to lock his two children in the wine cellar, and relentlessly beat his wife, demanding that she give him more respect. By the time the officers could subdue the raging captain, Madame Crunch lay unconscious, barely escaping being pummeled by a sock filled with crunch berries. On the way out the Captain reportedly screamed, "You'll learn to respect me, I be the Captain in this house." The Captain is currently undergoing psychiatric evaluation, and is awaiting trial in late March. Madame Crunch has filed for divorce and has been seen at the Honeycomb Hideout with the Silly Rabbit.

Another case in point is that of Lucky Charms. A bartender with whom we talked told us of a con man caught up in the fast life of cereal stardom. Known as Mr. Lucky, he used his fame and wealth in pursuit of high times and loose women. Any night of the week he could be found combing the bars of the Big Apple, looking for more than just a pot of gold. This type of behavior hasn't gone unnoticed. A General Mills executive, who wishes to remain anonymous, reported that on a number of occasions, Lucky showed up on the set with two women young enough to be his daughters, and the smell of whiskey on his breath. On top of all this, Lucky's problems worsened when Dublin's Saucy Films, Inc. announced that they would release a number of erotic films Lucky made when he was climbing the ladder of success. The first film, to be released on March 1, will be titled, "Lucky's Magic Wand of Love." Others will follow, including, "Lucky and the Kids," "Lucky Does Dublin," and the most shocking of them all, "Behind the Green Pants." Lucky seems to understand that he can't change his past, but he can change his future. Reportedly, he checked into the Tony Tiger rehab clinic and is undergoing treatment for various substance abuses.

Our last story involves none other than the beloved Toucan Sam. Unfortunately Sam is a bird gone utterly mad, a bird caught up in the fantasy world of LSD. Since his last commercial shoot in late 1989, Sam has been touring with the Grateful Dead, with a small group of acid-induced disciples, to whom he is known as "the Grand Wizard Sam." Feared by most Deadheads, Sam and his band of Tripping Fools terrify concertgoers by drinking vials of liquid and licking whole sheets of acid. Sam was recently arrested at the New Year's show at Oakland Coliseum for dancing naked on a police vehicle. While being questioned, Sam's only defense was, "oh the visuals, oh the wondrous visuals." When we talked to Jerry Garcia about how he felt he said, "It's people like the Grand Wizard Sam and his followers who give The Dead a bad name."

One question that we could never answer is: Why does cereal

stardom in particular lead to a life of self-abuse? Perhaps being suddenly thrown into the Saturday morning limelight along with being placed on breakfast tables across America can make even the humblest man feel invincible. But unfortunately this misconception is what eventually leads to their final fall from grace. We ask you to try to be understanding; they are merely a product of their environment. We assure you that they are wholeheartedly sorry for deceiving the American public. But we, as the generation who grew up believing in these characters, can't help but experience a feeling of loss. And that's the biggest tragedy of all.

So until next week, see if you can find some time to rent *Breakin' Two, Electric Boogaloo,* and remember, "We are the World, We are the Children."

DAVE BALTER is founder and CEO of Bzz-Agent, Inc., one of the world's first and most highly-respected word of mouth media companies—and certainly the most talked-about. Balter and BzzAgent were featured in a *New York Times Magazine* cover story in 2004, just two years after the company's founding, and have since been a regular presence in print, broadcast, online media, and Harvard Business School case studies.

BzzAgent has grown into a network of 400,000 volunteers who—just by talking to others and sharing their opinions—have helped more than 250 companies generate word of mouth about everything from sausages to social networks. In just six years, BzzAgent has generated more than 85 million dialogues for more than 450 brands.

Dave is a serial entrepreneur who started-up and sold two companies prior to creating BzzAgent. In 2004, he co-founded the Word of Mouth Marketing Association (WOMMA) and currently sits on its board of directors. In 2008, Harvard Business School dubbed him one of Boston's "Hottest Technology CEOs" and the Adclub named him a "Future Legend." Dave's first book, *Grapevine: How Buzz was a Fad and Word of Mouth is Forever,* was published by Portfolio, the business imprint of the Penguin Group, in 2005.

In some weird and virtually unexplainable twist of fate, Dave was named one of the "7 People Changing the Face of Beauty" by *Women's Wear Daily*—even though he has difficulty matching his socks.